# The Essential Survival Guide for the 21st Century

## God's Solutions to Life's Problems

Norman Fisher

*Getting to know God better
... a linked set of practical group
and individual studies*

paternoster
*Lifestyle*

First published in 2001
by Paternoster Lifestyle

07 06 05 04 03 02 01   7 6 5 4 3 2 1

Paternoster Lifestyle is an imprint of Paternoster Publishing
PO Box 300, Carlisle, Cumbria, CA3 0QS, UK
and Paternoster Publishing USA
Box 1047, Waynesboro, GA 30830-2047
www.paternoster-publishing.com

**British Library Cataloguing in Publication Data**

A catalogue record for this book is available from the British Library

## ISBN 1-85078-410-8

Designed and typeset by Temple DPS Ltd, Manchester

Printed in Great Britain by
Cox and Wyman, Cardiff Road, Reading, Berkshire.

# CONTENTS

# Foreword

I was not prepared for how much I would enjoy this book and how eagerly I would want to recommend it. This is mainly because it is so God-centred. So much theology today is man-centred, so many Bible studies are also written with little emphasis upon God's perspective, but Dr Fisher's work is one that sees things from God's point of view – all the way to the end.

Dr Norman Fisher is the Professor of Project Management at the University of Reading. His main purpose in writing this book is to stem the flow of new Christians out of the church. He believes that there is a way to keep new Christians once they have been won. Statistics show, sadly, that 90% of new Christians give up on their newfound faith within two years. Norman sees his own book as being a tool that can be used by churches who have a vigorous evangelism programme but which can also be used in universities, prisons, with youth groups, small groups and also in the workplace. It is especially for those from a non-church culture. Although it is aimed at the 18-35 year old, it is most suitable for maturer Christians as well.

The book is full of very practical and readable illustrations. They are absolutely wonderful. I myself was gripped by his attacking theistic evolutionary views on the basis that, if Jesus could make the best wine at the end of the wedding in Cana, meaning that it was aged wine, how easily God could create the world as old! God does this that we might believe by faith – not by science or by sight. I find this so essential to today's trend against believing in the biblical account of creation.

Norman emphasises how much God wants a close relationship with us. There's a strong emphasis on getting to know God intimately, and he emphasises Scripture memorisation as a way to achieve this kind of intimacy. He sees this also as a great tool against attacks of the devil in one's life.

What we have in this book, then, is truly an essential guide for Christians to survive in the twenty-first century. He shows the basics of Christianity with particular reference to studying such in ten weeks. You may feel a little bit intimidated by how much is required, including spending thirty minutes a day in prayer. However, I was brought up to believe that every Christian should spend thirty minutes a day in prayer and I have emphasised that in my own church for twenty-five years. Those who set this as a goal – and do it – will never be sorry! However, Norman gives good help in this area as to how to spend the thirty minutes each day.

It is my prayer that this book will have wide acceptance, that it will be used in countless groups all over Britain and that Norman's vision to stem the tide of Christians leaving the church will be realised. The wider the acceptance of this book, the greater will be the growth of the church – not to mention the honour of God.

**R.T. Kendall**
*Westminster Chapel*
*London*
*July 2001*

# Introduction

## HOW IT WORKS

The *Essential Survival Guide* (ESG) is a set of studies based on the need to get the fundamentals of the traditional Christian faith understood by new believers in a way that most will find challenging, stimulating but not too difficult. The study series is pitched at someone who has made a decision to become a Christian and who has been through a basic course leading to baptism or church membership.

The study series is Bible based and has been designed to be used by a range of different church groups and is deliberately non-denominational. It is based for convenience around the 'cell group' and the 'underground' cell church concept. The idea is that anyone who has successfully completed the ten-week series, should be encouraged as the next step in their own Christian life, to lead their own ESG course for ten weeks *as soon as possible*. It should be remembered that in the Apostle Paul's time, many church elders/leaders had often been a Christian for less than a year. The benchmark was then and should be now, not age, nor 'length of service', social position, education (or lack of it), a close chum of the senior pastor/church leader, or 'grand' public experiences. Rather it should be real deep spiritual growth and maturity, that has been proved, tested in situations over a suitable period of time, all of which should act as a confirmation of God's anointing for the role of leader.

Thus exponential growth in numbers by *division* is what is sought. So that within every ten or twelve weeks each of the 6-10 ESG group members who have completed the course successfully, are in turn leading their own group of 6-10. In addition the aim is to pass on experience, knowledge, revelation and wisdom about practical, down-to-earth, *real* Christian living. The vision is to achieve this in a *cascade* fashion, so as to prepare and equip the next group of cell group leaders.

## ACKNOWLEDGEMENTS

The concept and the material contained in the series has grown and developed over many years and early drafts have been developed and widely tested over the last six to seven years or so. I am indebted to a range of godly men and women for the privilege of learning from them or being taught by them. In addition the material is eclectic in that I have subconsciously drawn on the writings, wisdom and revelation of many. In addition God has put many in the right place at the right time, to offer material and ideas as well as wise and much-needed advice. Amongst the very many a few stand out: David Pawson, Dr Francis Schaeffer, Mr and Mrs H. Kraushaar, Phillip Cheale, Eric Bird, Colin Dye, Colin Urquart, Dr Martin Lloyd-Jones, Sam Larbie and Dr R.T. Kendall.

In addition I am grateful for the support of the Rev. Bernard Thompson and the elders and many members of The Ridgeway Community Church past and present, in particular to Ted Ripley and His wife Vi (who sadly died before seeing the finished study), who have tested the course out on numerous groups of new Christians. The feedback has allowed me to amend and develop the course. Also to John Twine for his careful proofreading and checking of an early draft.

I am grateful to Julia my wife and my two sons for their ideas, encouragement and support.

*Norman Fisher*
*May 2001*

# The Concept

This series of short studies will look at what the Bible says about the problems and issues of life and how to deal with them: that is, the sort of things that we will all face as we deal with the various stages of everyday life. Many may be surprised to know that despite the fact that the Bible was written two thousand or more years ago, what it has to say is relevant, is up to date and above all is very practical and applicable to the issues of living today.

This set of studies attempts to provide both a fair and a balanced view of what the Bible teaches. The Bible is God's 'workshop manual', like a car workshop manual, for every practical aspect of life. It has instructions, help and advice for each stage of living. It tells each of us how to cope with issues, problems and the challenges of life. It even has stories, some historically accurate and others (parables) simply to illustrate the dos and don'ts. The stories (case studies) are often amazingly candid and revealing, often describing inspiring success or devastating failure.

How the Bible is viewed by the person studying it is important. As the inspired word of God, it should be approached in a childlike but not a childish way. It helps us understand God. It helps us understand who Jesus and the Holy Spirit are and in addition how we should approach both the big and the small issues of everyday life.

Neither those who have prepared the studies, nor those who lead them from time to time, should consider themselves to be experts or indeed any better at coping with life! None should believe that they have a 'monopoly on truth', or a 'private

1

telephone line' to God. Possibly the study leaders have 'fallen over' in life and had to 'pick themselves up' a little more often, and have had a little more time to study the Bible. But we are all learning. Together we are all trying to discover and apply the Bible principles for the issues of life in the 21st Century.

## THE STRUCTURE OF THIS SERIES OF STUDIES

The Bible study series is made up of a number of interrelated but standalone modules, each focused on a different aspect of God, or how He views things. The components of the series are:

1. Which God do we worship?
2. How do we know what God is like?
3. The nature of the God we worship.
4. A loving caring God?
5. The true nature of man – God's view!
6. Sin – an outdated concept?
7. Jesus – a man, God, or both?
8. Jesus rose bodily from the dead – so what does it mean?
9. The Holy Spirit and the Second Coming.
10. The relevance of the Bible plus practical matters.

## STUDYING THE BIBLE – HOW DO I DO IT?

The sort of Bible study covered in this series is designed to be well within the capability of all. It has been tested and refined over several years on a large number of people, of both genders and a wide range of age, social and educational backgrounds.

Some simple skills may need to be learned and the study leader can help you develop and practise them. You need a Bible in modern everyday English, one that you personally are comfortable with – unless of course you regularly speak

Shakespearean English at home! Translations of the Bible that are particularly recommended are: *New Living Translation* (NLT) published by Tyndale and the *New International Version* (NIV) published by Hodder & Stoughton. Finally and most important you need the help and guidance of God the Holy Spirit to help you to unlock the truths contained within the pages of the Bible. Your study leader will discuss this stage with you and help you to pray about it.

There are a number of simple rules or 'tips' that experienced Bible students have identified that can help you study the Bible effectively and make it both interesting, inspiring and perhaps at times gripping. They are:

1. It is of the utmost importance that you approach the Bible with a reverent attitude. You should regard the Bible as the unique inspired word of God and not just as another book, or a 'special work' of literature, or just history, or like other 'Holy Books'. But don't worship the Bible; rather 'unpack' it, that is, find out what it contains inside for you today.

2. The Bible should be studied as eagerly as a hungry or thirsty man seeks for food or water. What you personally get out of studying the Bible will almost certainly be in direct proportion to the effort that you (not your church leader or Bible study leader) put in to your study and the prayer by you and others that surrounds it.

3. It is always good to learn from an experienced Bible teacher that God has anointed, but there is something extra and more than a little special, exciting or inspiring about a word from the Lord, a truth, an insight, or a principle, that you have discovered for yourself under the guidance of the Holy Spirit.

4. It is often helpful to see Bible study as a 'lifetime' journey, perhaps a bit like exploring a large city or country. Treat Bible study as a quest or as a pilgrimage, where you wish to

3

seek personal first-hand knowledge of the vast truths of the Christian faith, of visions, of things to come, of inspiration and instruction for life. Also it is good to learn from the colourful case studies of life – in both the Old and New Testaments, whether historically accurate accounts or illustrative parables. Try to obtain a broad (rather than a narrow) view of Scripture, as it will help you keep a balanced view of your Christian faith. A London 'cabby' (taxi driver) can take two years or longer to learn 'the knowledge', that is learn by heart how to navigate round the capital city from point to point without a map. A 'cabby' will tell you that the delight of passing 'the test' and obtaining the 'licence' makes all the hard work worthwhile. Will not 'the delight' be all the greater for the Christian, as he or she begins to see his or her knowledge of the Bible growing?

5. 'Study Scripture as a miner might dig out a seam of gold.' As with nuggets of gold, most great truths do not lie as it were on the surface waiting to be casually picked up. It is more often by patient, careful and diligent study and searching of Scripture, prayer and discussions with other Christians, that they can be found, taken possession of, understood and applied to the practical problems of everyday living.

## SOME SIMPLE TECHNIQUES

Reading a few verses of Scripture each day as part of a regular time spent with God, perhaps using 'daily Bible notes', can be very helpful indeed. However it should be clear that such activity really is no substitute for proper (systematic) study of the Scriptures. The Bible tells us that for each of us, there comes a point when we must stop eating baby food and move onto real (adult) food, if we are to grow and develop as Christians. What the Bible means by this, is that we must undertake regular systematic Bible study if we are to achieve the normal Christian life.

Briefly described below are five simple study techniques, that you might find useful.

1. Try to study a **whole book** of the Bible and attempt to master it, by ascertaining its author and reading about the background to it in a suitable reference book.[1] Establish who the book was originally aimed at, why and when it was written, its purpose and its main teaching. A useful start is to obtain a cassette or video tape recording of 'book overviews' by for example David Pawson.[2]

2. Plan and study particular chapters of books and **important passages** of Scripture as a project on its own. Familiarise yourself with the well-known but often important passages and attempt to understand the message or principle that they contain.

3. Identify and then follow a **particular topic**: that is, select a subject or a theme and trace it through the Bible. For this you will probably need one or more of several types of reference/study aids.[3] See your study leader if you are not familiar with this type of publication.

4. Select and study a **Bible character**, by reading and studying all that Scripture says about him or her. For example in the Old Testament you could study the life of Abraham, David or Esther; in the New Testament perhaps Peter, John the Baptist, or Mary the mother of Jesus.

5. Memorise a number of **key Bible verses**, so that they may be available to you in an emergency, or whenever a need may arise. The memorising of Bible verses puts both offensive and defensive weapons into the hands of a Christian. Many experienced Christians testify to the effectiveness of this technique in the struggle against a particular temptation, or when dealing with a big personal issue, such as depression, worry, anxiety or panic attacks. There are several very good tried and tested systems on the market: for example, the *Topical Memory System* published by The Navigators is excellent.[4]

Generally there are a large number of books available on prayer, which will depend largely on experience and personal preference. Two good examples are: [5] and [6].

Finally, by way of introduction, your study leader will discuss with you and attempt to answer any preliminary questions that you may have. Now read Deuteronomy Chapter 6 in a modern version of the Bible.

## Reference notes

1 Alexander, D. and Alexander, P., (1999), *The New Lion Handbook to the Bible*, Lion Publishing, Tring Herts., ISBN: 0745938701. Also: Unger M.F., (1998), New Unger's Bible Handbook, Moody, ISBN: 0802490492.

2 A full list of the David Pawson (and other) recordings can be obtained from Anchor Recordings, 72 The Street, Kennington, Ashford, Kent, TN24 9HS UK.

3 A very large number of reference study books exist, such as Bible commentaries, concordances and reference systems such as that of the 'Thompson Chain Reference Edition'. For further help in this area ask your study leader, Church leader or at a Christian Book Shop. For example: Bruce, F.F., New International Bible Commentary, Zondervan, ISBN: 0310220203.
Pawson, D., (1999), *Unlocking the Bible Vol. 1*, Marshall Pickering, ISBN: 0551031875.
Pawson D., (1999), *Hope for the Millennium*, Hodder and Stoughton, ISBN: 0340735597.

4 The *Topical Memory System* is published by Navpress – A Ministry of The Navigators (Biblical reference: SPCN 9 – 90073 – 369 – X). It is obtainable through your local Christian Bookshop.

5 Ramon SSF, Brother, (1995), *The Heart of Prayer*, HarperCollins, London, ISBN: 0551029072; Ramon SSF, Brother, (1998), The Prayer Mountain, Canterbury Press, ISBN: 1853112259.

6 Dye, Colin, (1998), *Prayer That Gets Answers*, Dovewell Publications, London (ISBN 1 898 444 75 7).

# AN OVERVIEW TO
# THE TEN-WEEK SERIES

This course consists of nine individual study units and will take place over a ten-week period.

Week 1 will consist of the following activities:

1. An introduction to basic Bible study.

2. An explanation of how and why the help of the Holy Spirit should be sought through prayer when undertaking Bible study.

3. An overview of the subject to be covered in this course and how the various components of it will work.

4. A discussion of weekly group tasks.

5. A discussion of weekly individual tasks.

6. A group Bible study on 'Who is God?'

7. An opportunity to ask questions about the week's individual tasks.

Weeks 2-9 will consist of the following activities:

1. A brief discussion on how each member in turn 'got on' with their *individual* tasks, in particular with prayer and the memory verse.

2. Each week the study leader will go through the 'individual' study task to ascertain how successful each participant has been. The emphasis and purpose is to encourage, train,

improve and equip. It is not to 'check up' on or to embarrass participants. It is important however that the study leader will need to be satisfied that the study is being undertaken properly, and that participants are not struggling or discouraged! Each member will be expected to discuss what he/she has discovered from the Bible study.

3. A discussion on the next individual task.

4. An opportunity to ask questions.

Week 10 will consist of the following tasks:

1. The study leader will go through the last 'individual study'. Each member will be expected to discuss what he/she has personally discovered from the Bible study.

2. A concluding summarising Bible study led by the group leader.

3. A discussion on what you have learned, the way forward in terms of spiritual growth e.g. 'What next?'

The ten-week course will deal with nine units of 'individual' study and two group studies (weeks 1 and 10).

They are:

1. Which God do we worship?
2. How do we know what God is like?
3. The nature of the God we worship.
4. A loving caring God.
5. The true nature of man – God's view!
6. Sin – an outdated concept?
7. Jesus – a man, God or both?
8. Jesus rose bodily from the dead – so what does it mean?
9. The Holy Spirit and the Second Coming.
10. The relevance of the Bible.

A reasonable guide to the time needed to be spent is that the individual tasks listed above should take each day about one to one and a half hours of your time over a one-week period. If this seems onerous, reflect on how many hours a day you spend watching television (e.g. news, soaps or sport)!

The arrangements for how the daily time is spent, in one session or broken into two or three over the day, will depend on the circumstances of the participant.

# Week 1:
# WHICH GOD DO WE
# WORSHIP?

## GROUP WORK SECTION

Today there are many different ideas about God. It may therefore seem impossible to say anything certain or reliable about him. After all, no one has ever seen God!

A good place at which to start a discussion about God is with the world around us and the universe itself! It is there – its existence poses a rather basic question: 'How did it get there?' Currently there are four different answers that are most commonly referred to:

1. Some rather extreme philosophers suggest that it is not there at all! The whole thing is a figment of the mind, an illusion, a sort of bad dream. For example, they suggest that matter does not exist!

2. Others argue that the universe has always been there, but has changed, developed and evolved. Modern science makes this explanation an increasingly difficult one to defend. An increasing number of scientists are supporting the explanation that the universe had a beginning and will have an end! The popular scientific view held by astrophysicists is called the 'big bang' theory and most currently believe it happened between three billion and 12,000 billion years ago depending on the evolutionary timescales they try to fit in! These scientists believe that the universe started at a precise point (a big bang) and will end at a precise point (another big bang!). But even this explanation is currently being challenged by mathematicians who believe that just before the big bang (the point of creation), the Universe was the size of a pea, suspended in a timeless void. The mathematicians suggest a start but no end, that the Universe will continue to grow (expand) for ever. Scientists arrive at this sort of thinking by first looking at all of the (hard) evidence available and then constructing an explanation that 'fits' the

evidence. When new evidence or data becomes available, the current explanation can be tested to see if it is still adequate. If not, it will then be refined. Many scientists and in many fields of scientific study, are often painfully aware that their 'current explanations' are not really adequate. They await a gifted colleague to devise a better and often radically different scientific explanation. This process reveals both the strength and the weakness of modern science. The strength is that this approach allows rapid growth in our understanding in many areas of science such as medicine, materials and biology, because everything is up for challenge within the 'public domain'. However, the weakness is that the current scientific explanation will be revised and is therefore 'not cast in tablets of stone', a point that is easily forgotten. Yet we should remember that the principles and truths of Scripture are that they are from God and therefore do not need to change as man's understanding increases or meets modern fashions. The principles and truths on the original 'tablets of stone', are just as relevant today as they were when Moses brought them down from Mount Sinai (Exodus 31:18 and 34: 29-32). This was the beginning of a covenant relationship that God began with the Jews. As Christians today we have a different kind of relationship with God: grace and mercy through Jesus. This has been built on the first relationship with the Jews, but more of that later!

3. The third school of thought or explanation is based on the idea of chance. At some remote time/point in history nothing became something, and we had a spontaneous creation that has led to what we see around us today. No explanation is given by the supporters of this view for where the initial matter came from.

4. The fourth answer is the biblical and traditional Christian view; that is, the world was created – it had a beginning, at a

13

point in time and space. The very fact of its existence is proof it is argued that there must be a power and an intelligence greater than the universe, which willed (or created) its existence. It is this awesome power and awesome intelligence that is the being to whom Christians give the title God. This view holds up to scrutiny much better than many imagine or believe. For example Jewish/Christian records suggest that the world is much younger than is currently suggested by many scientists. *'What about fossils?'* scientists ask, *'surely that suggests that the Christian view is wrong?'*. To answer this we must not restrict the actions of God to what is considered possible to the human mind. For example, when Jesus created the wine from water at Cana in Galilee (John 2:1-10), He produced wine of a very high standard, probably in seconds, of a quality that in the normal course of events would have taken many months or perhaps years to ferment and mature – read the story! If analysed scientifically, the results would have suggested that the wine was very much older than in fact it was! Remember, the same God that created the wine created the world. And He created a world younger than its apparent age, a going concern that was perfect. He inspired the writers of the various books of the Bible to record the events. That is, God told them what to write down. Meanwhile, many scientists from different disciplines are turning to Scripture for evidence of origins.

**Question**: What do you think?

So what does the Bible say about this super intelligent/ powerful being? Holding the traditional Christian biblical view it is possible to list some of the more obvious *truths* about God:

– He is a Being of great power at a level well outside of our comprehension.

– He is a Being of phenomenal intelligence, again well outside of our comprehension.

14

- He is a God of variety and wonderful artistry.

- He cares about fine detail, again in a way that we cannot comprehend.

- He is on His own – there is no other 'creative mind' at work in our universe.

In Genesis Chapter 1 the Bible describes this being ... 'God'.

? **Question**: What does it tell the reader about His character?

? **Question**: What sort of relationship did God want with man? (Genesis 3:8-24)

? **Question**: Is this a scientific or is it a theological account of the act of creation? What is the difference? For example, how would you explain how a computer works or how an aircraft flies – to a five- or six-year-old child?

📖 *Reading: Aspects of God's character can be discovered in Exodus 3:1-11(a), 20:1-18, 21.*

? **Question**: Why were Abimeleck and His officials afraid? (Genesis 20:8-10)

? **Question**: Was it necessary for God's people to understand these aspects of His character? Why?

? **Question**: How important is it to know about God today?

📖 *Reading: List the different ways used to describe God in Psalms 91, 99, 100:5 and 102.*

❓ **Question**: What other ways of describing God's character come to mind as a result of reading these verses?

❓ **Question**: Do any of the ways that you have listed *seem* to contradict each other? How can this be explained?

📖 *Reading: Jesus teaches about God in Matthew 6; John 3; 4:24; 5:16-30 and 14:1-11.*

❓ **Question**: How relevant is this teaching to people you know?

## PREPARATION FOR THIS WEEK'S INDIVIDUAL TASK

There are four tasks for you to undertake on your own during the first week of this study series. They are:

1. *Individual Bible study*. This will help you develop further your understanding of what the Bible tells us about who God is. Work through the study and be ready to share your answers, doubts, questions and conclusions with your group next week.

2. *Individual prayer target*. Try and spend at least 20-30 minutes a day in prayer. Draw up a list of prayer topics and structure them on the basis of JOY: **J**esus (worship God and Jesus – thank both God and Jesus for what they have done for you); **O**thers (their needs); **Y**ourself (your concerns and needs).

16

Then spend some time each day, just being quiet before God, listen to Him, thinking and praying about areas of the Bible study that have particularly challenged you. Try and explore the difference between saying (a list of) prayers and praying (communicating with God, in particular letting Him speak to you). Try and have a 'conversation' with God whilst doing the 'tasks of the day'. Remember, though it may not always seem so, *Jesus has promised that He, in the form of the Holy Spirit, is with you and in you all the time*. Discuss this with your group leader.

3. *Fast and pray*. Try and *'fast and pray'* for one day before the next group meeting. It is important to discuss how to do this with your group leader before attempting it.

4. *Memorise a verse of Scripture*. Do this so that you can recite it from memory at the next meeting. Discuss this with your group leader also.

A suggested memory verse for the week: 1 John 1:9.

A reasonable guide is that the individual tasks listed above should take **each day** about one hour plus of your time in total: not necessarily 60 minutes all at once, but the hour can be made up of time taken at a number of quiet moments during the day. However it is recommended that each morning, first thing, some time is spent alone with God. Remember, to listen to God and to talk to him, you need space/quiet, even if only for a small amount of time each day. Remember, that after His conversion and an initial bit of enthusiasm, Paul went off into the stillness of the desert of Arabia to sort things out with God. Paul knew Psalm 62:5. Jesus battled with Satan alone in the desert and God spoke to and challenged Moses and Amos in the stillness of a desert, not in a busy town or a lively University. Before Paul, Moses or even Jesus faced the day-to-day bustle and pressure of the task that God had given them, they first had to get things sorted out with God in the empty silent desert! The principle is clear, we all need space, time and quietness to hear God, perhaps in a bedroom, or a quiet room in a church complex: it does not have to be a desert!

(If you think that an hour is too long – that it is too large a daily commitment, consider or even make a note of how long each day you spend watching television – the news, a television soap, or sport. Are the TV programmes you watch that good? How much do you really want to get to know God?)

## INDIVIDUAL WORK SECTION

This section is for individual study. Your conclusions should be written down. Your answers, queries and questions will be discussed at the next group meeting, as will those of other group members.

?    **Question**: How do we know that God exists?

?    **Question**: How can we find out what He is like?

?    **Question**: God wants a relationship with each of us! He has revealed Himself in a way that we can relate to! How has He made communication with Himself possible?

?    **Question**: How can we find out more about God?

Each of the above questions or statements will be dealt with in this study.

### SO WHICH GOD DO WE WORSHIP?

Mankind since the beginning of time has assumed that knowledge about the purpose of our existence and knowledge about supernatural beings can be obtained by thought, debate and study.

Brilliant men of most great civilisations, for example the ancient Greeks, have struggled, searched and come to conclusions only to be contradicted by the thoughts of the next great mind. Sometimes their ideas are optimistic, believing that man is slowly moving towards a better world, built on education, democracy, human rights, good applications of science and technology. Others are pessimistic, sometimes leading to despair or radical social or political action.

The philosopher and Christian Francis Schaefer, once showed two films of the same incident. It was a film of a demonstration that ended in a violent confrontation between demonstrators and police. Film version (a) had been edited by someone sympathetic to the police, with cameras positioned *behind* police lines. The viewer would quickly develop sympathy for the police who were 'clearly' trying to do a difficult job with violent protesters. Film version (b) had a similar camera *behind* the demonstrators and the sympathy of the film editor lay with the demonstrators. The same incident, but this time the viewer saw peaceful protesters attacked by 'fascist' police, who were using quite unnecessary force!! The conclusion that you came to about the incident was largely dictated by the position of the camera and the sympathies of the film editor. In just the same way, ideas about the purpose of man's existence and ideas about God, depend upon your starting point and who has influenced your thinking – that is your starting presupposition or values! As a result, two brilliant and utterly sincere minds can draw radically different conclusions about the same incident or *seemingly objective* version of history.

To try and get some understanding of how big God is and how much of Him is beyond our comprehension, imagine that you are an ant, a worker ant, a member of a large hardworking colony. You have your personal skills, territory and responsibilities. You have your own friends, work colleagues and set of young to look after, food to prepare and the quarters you live in to repair, clean and extend. You are busy doing all of this working in an ant 'time frame'. Your ant equivalent of your allocated 'three score years and ten' life span, is in fact in a human time frame just a few days.

At a point in your life, quite unexpectedly, a large part of your colony is suddenly lifted up into the air, moved and dropped violently by a large powerful shiny metallic object. To you, the being (a man) behind this action and his spade, are quite beyond your understanding. You are a practical and caring ant and your immediate concern is for the safety of your charges and yourself – looking at the events from an 'ant's world view'. As you are attempting to cope with these traumatic and unexpected events, the sole of a large rubber boot thunders down with great force and crushes another large part of the colony – 'your cosy world', the only world that you know. You do not see or understand the gardener, a man, a caring husband, a loving father; all you are aware of is the spade and the rubber boot, neither of which you have any concept of or understand; or how and why they have invaded your world – an 'ant's-eye view' of the bigger world.

The ant at a lower level of existence with his world-view cannot relate to, comprehend or communicate with the gardener or his world. If it were possible for the man and the ant to communicate, it is possible that gradually the ant would begin to understand little bits of the gardener and his actions in terms of his world etc. But no such method exists.

The Bible tells us that humans have been made in the image of God and have been equipped with the skills and tools necessary to communicate: that is ears, eyes, a brain, language and the ability to learn, look and listen, amongst other things. But there is another problem for the ant. Even if ants could communicate such that one ant observed the spade and another the rubber boot, there would be an argument about the nature of the gardener. Each had observed a different aspect of his actions – whose ideas would be correct? Of course they could combine their knowledge, but only if they could hear and understand the gardener's voice would they be in a position to begin to know the truth and combine their knowledge from the correct starting point!

God has made us able to receive the truth about Himself, but only as He chooses to reveal it to us.

### THE ONLY ACCURATE AND RELIABLE SOURCE OF OUR KNOWLEDGE OF GOD – IS GOD HIMSELF

📖 *Read: Genesis 1:1; John 1:1 and Colossians 1:15-18.*

❓ **Question**: Who was involved in the work of creating the earth and the rest of the universe?

❓ **Question**: Why was the earth and the rest of the universe created?

❓ **Question**: Did God invent time as we know it?

21

It is important as part of knowing which God we worship to realise that:

1. Both physical and non-physical things were created by God.

2. Time was created by God.

3. God alone existed prior to creation.

4. Creation was purpose-built by God and centred on man.

God is so different from us, that unless He reveals Himself to us we can only begin to guess as to what He is really like.

📖 *Read: Exodus 24:17; Isaiah 40:12-31; 55:8-13; Psalm 90; Matthew 19:7; Luke 2:9; Romans 2:4.*

In these passages God reveals Himself in different ways – in word format (for the ear) and in picture format (for the eye). Our minds can receive information from both ear and eye and build up a picture of what God is like, but solely on the basis of what He has revealed to us.

Man, no matter how clever, how well informed or educated, *without revelation from God*, can no more understand His nature or what He is like or His purposes, than the ant in the example above can understand the nature and purpose of a gardener!

### THE SOURCE OF OUR KNOWLEDGE OF GOD IS GOD HIMSELF ALONE

📖 *Read: Isaiah 40:12-31; 55:8-13; Psalm 90*

？ **Question**: What facet of God's character do we discover in the passages from Isaiah and Psalm 90?

？ **Question**: Which verses show:

1. God's limitless intelligence ?

2. His incomprehensible power and greatness?

3. The nature and immensity of His love?

4. His profound wisdom?

？ **Question**: What do we discover about the nature of mankind in the Isaiah passages above?

？ **Questions**: Which verses show:

1. Man's relative lack of understanding and limitations?

2. Man's over-inflated sense of his own understanding?

3. Man's relative insignificance within the known universe?

4. Man's hopeless attempts at understanding God?

📖 *Read: Job 38.*

？ **Questions**:

1. What does Job 38 tell us about man's knowledge and understanding of the enormity of God? Why can we not challenge Him on this?

2. Some of the words, expressions and pictures painted in Job 38, are not easy to understand for the modern scientifically trained or influenced mind.

3. Does this devalue them, or rather does it put into context how little man really knows?

4. What is the real message behind this picture language?

📖 *Read: Matthew 11:25-30; Psalm 145:13, 2 Peter 3:8; Psalm 18:35; 1 John 3:1; Psalm 103:11 and Psalm 34:18.*

❓ **Question**: What do these readings tell us about God's character?

📖 *Read: Ezekiel 1:4-28.*

❓ **Question**: What is the overall impression created by the verses in Ezekiel?

We must realise that although He is close to us, a loving and gentle father, He is nevertheless immeasurably great and that we are small. *Arguing* with Him is as useful as the ant with the man (see Isaiah 25:6-8; 45:20-23). This is a difficult concept to grasp, as to begin to understand God as He wants us to, we must first come to terms with all the facets of His personality. Jesus summed it up in Matthew 5:36 and 6:27. Some facets are more difficult to come to terms with than others. The temptation is to exclude the ones that don't fit into our ideas about God. We must strongly resist this!

Given the gulf between the immensity of God and the smallness of man, there can be no other way. Unlike the ant and the gardener digging the vegetable plot, between whom communication is not possible, we have been created in such a way that it is possible for us to have fellowship with God. Communication with God is possible – it is up to us to obtain *'the telephone link'* that God has created and given to us and to learn how to use it.

## A SUMMARY OF THE POINTS DISCUSSED SO FAR

The key points so far are summed up in the three questions below that you should ask yourself. They are:

1. Have I read carefully and understood the Scripture passages listed?

2. What are the key issues identified in these passages?

3. Are there any issues raised that I have difficulty with? If I have, then why?

? **Question**: Could I explain what I have learned so far to others if they asked questions about why I regard the Bible so highly: To an adult neighbour? To a young teenager?

# Week 2:
# HOW DO WE KNOW WHAT GOD IS LIKE?

## GROUP WORK SECTION

This week will consist of a brief discussion on how each member 'got on' with their individual tasks. They were:

1. Prayer/fasting

2. The memory verse (1 John 1:9)

3. Individual Bible study

After this your study leader will then go through last week's 'individual study' entitled 'Which God do we worship?' He or she will ask each to discuss the answers they have given and the conclusions reached. This will involve general discussion as the review proceeds.

The leader will then outline the individual tasks for next week. They are:

1. Individual Bible study that will help you to develop further your understanding of what the Bible tells us of what God is like. Again work through the study and be ready to share your answers and conclusions next week.

2. Individual prayer target. Try and spend at least 20-30 minutes each day in prayer. Develop a suitable structure for your prayer list. Again try and fast for one day before the next group meeting. Perhaps fast over a specific issue or prayer request.

3. Memorise a new verse of Scripture: John 16:33

## INDIVIDUAL WORK SECTION

This section is for individual study. Your conclusions should be written down. Your answers, queries and questions will be discussed at the next group meeting, as will those of other group members.

There are two key ways in which God has revealed Himself to mankind – through His creation and through the Bible. We will look first at His creation.

## GOD REVEALS HIMSELF TO HUMANITY THROUGH HIS CREATION

Many excellent nature or natural history programmes on television talk about evolution as if it were a proven scientific fact beyond scientific doubt, also about 'nature' as if it were a thinking creative person and often female. This can be illustrated by recent quote from such a programme: *'Nature has equipped these birds to survive immense desert heat ... she has developed for the bird a plumage that deflects heat and allows the brooding birds to protect their eggs and later chicks from the strong rays of the sun.'* Using natural abilities of observation, even humanist man has to marvel at what he observes in the 'created world'. However he must invent (reinvent?) a 'mother nature', an ancient and man-made explanation/description of God, as presumably he cannot bring himself to accept that there is a creating God beyond his comprehension and powers of deduction. Such a change of view for humanist man would have profound implications for his 'world-view', his personal life and the way he lives it. For many this would be humbling in terms of reputation and costly in terms of life style!

Yet it is worth remembering that everything man has made, often to his peers very complex, clever and at times awesome, he has made in the end with things around him, things he has found. However the Bible and increasingly astrophysicists tell us that in the beginning there was nothing. Scientists talk about a point (in time and space?) when there was for want of a better description 'a big bang', when nothing was split into positive and negative matter e.g. $0 = 2 + (-2)$. The Bible says that out of the big black void that we call space, came the voice of God saying *'Let there be light'*; immediately, the void was filled (the big bang?). Out of nothing God created the stars and the galaxies (the heavens and the earth). Whilst all of this was happening, God formed and breathed on one particular planet, and what we know as planet Earth began. He took the energy created and formed them into galaxies and from these stars and stars, planets. Later as the stars with their attendant planets burn out they collapse in on themselves (implode – become negative matter). As a large star burns out it cools, and at a certain point implodes sucking into itself positive (known) matter. This is what scientists call a black hole (negative matter) – a bit like a plug hole in a bath sucking into itself the bath water. Modern research scientists are beginning to detect negative matter. Several leading researchers are suggesting that we can only observe/see/measure about 10% of what is out there in the universe. Thus we can begin to understand just a little of what God did: what is described in the Bible – in non-scientific language.

So much for the big picture, what about the smaller picture? For example, if you look through a microscope you can observe a 'micro world' of amazing complexity and beauty. You can observe how life as God created it is self-regulating (the balance in God's creation) and self-perpetuating (the preservation of the species). All of this is a demonstration of the wonder and amazing goodness and wisdom of God. This leaves the question then, *'If all of this is so, why do not those making natural history programmes, almost certainly gifted, intellectually honest people, come to the same conclusion as the Bible, that an amazing God of wisdom and goodness created the world?'* To answer this, we need to look at the frailty of mankind, all mankind even the best. In reality the scientific concept of objectivity, if we are really honest, rarely if ever exists, other than in perhaps the most simple experiments of the foundational sciences. Clearly, levels of individual bias are easier to measure than that of collective bias. Each of us starts our observations with a presupposition, an individual world-view, a personal opinion/position, a personal agenda, motives or value system. This bias leads many scientists to want to discount God's existence and act of creation.

The elimination of observer bias, individual or collective, is a difficult concept. How would we know when we had achieved it? To achieve it we would need to be able to measure against a reliable and truly objective 'benchmark'. This 'benchmark' for Christians is the revelation of God. The conclusion remains that without God's revelation, observer bias taints or influences our observations.

Modern philosophers tell us that we are now in an age when each of our 'world-views', our opinions, are as good or as valid as those of any other human being. From the human perspective this is the obvious, equitable and natural result of both democracy, equality and human rights. However the Bible warns us that this is a wrong approach. By comparison with God, we have as much wisdom or knowledge as an ant. As clever as mankind may be, we have got man's knowledge and achievements out of proportion with reality. How well have we managed what we have around us? We may be able to clone an animal, grow a human ear in a laboratory, observe galaxies that *appear* to be 7-8 billion light years away; but look at the mess we are also making of the world around us. For example, it was suggested just before and after World War II that the

31

Indian Ocean alone could feed the whole of the world's population – if properly harvested. Yet today, it stands over-fished by probably as few as two of the world's nations! So we have wars, pollution, tyranny, hunger, disease and shortages of water on an increasingly global scale. Current world economic conditions offer us little comfort. Look at the examples of genocide and other instances of man's inhumanity to man in the 1990s alone!

All of this points us to the fact that the world and the heavens around us are the handiwork of an intelligent and purposeful creator. The atheist, the humanist, the secularist, hang on to a belief in man and his ideas such as evolution, simply because he has or wants nothing else. A less charitable view is that he has deliberately chosen not to believe in God the creator. The Bible says however that he who truly seeks the one true God will find him. To him who knocks (God's door) it **will** be opened!

? **Question**: find one or more references in the Bible to the promise that those who truly seek the one true God will find him.

### Facing up to God's revelation through creation

📖 *Read: Psalm 19; Isaiah 40:25-26; Amos 4:13; Jeremiah 10:16 and Colossians 1:16.*

? **Question**: What do the writers of the various books of the Bible expect our reaction to God's creation to be?

The apostle Paul and his companion and friend Barnabas, were in a town called Lystra (Acts 14:8-20) preaching to the population who had not heard about the one true God. He described God as Creator, Sustainer and Provider, and made the point that He has 'not left Himself without witness'.

📖 *Read: Romans 1:18-32.*

❓ **Qustion**: Paul argues that the suppression of the truth of God's 'eternal power and deity' creates guilt, leaves men without any excuse, causes God to be angry and leads to sin and the breakdown of society. How should we react?

❓ **Question**: Is the theory of evolution as described in a typical school syllabus or as portrayed on popular television perhaps just a convenient modern way of denying God's existence?

It is interesting to note that a growing number of leading scientists consider the Evolution Theory as an unsatisfactory explanation of how the world around us got there! If you wish to pursue this subject further read *Evidence For Truth: Science*, by Victor Pearce, Eagle Publishing.

❓ **Question**: Can you see the hand of God in creation? Are you able to marvel at its beauty and give Him thanks?

*BUT ... THERE ARE THINGS WE CANNOT KNOW ABOUT GOD BY OBSERVING NATURE*

There are things we cannot know about God, merely by looking at the natural world, however wonderful it is. We cannot know that He is interested in each individual person or in every detail of creation. We cannot know that He has made absolute standards of right and wrong – **moral** laws which govern morally responsible beings. We cannot know that He has provided a way for us to know Him personally, to be loved by Him and to love Him in return. Nor can we know the severity of His justice as it condemns those who deliberately choose to ignore Him, deny Him and rebel against Him. We can only know these things as God speaks to us in human language. From the very beginning of human history He has done just this. God was speaking and has continued to speak. The Bible is the record of God progressively revealing Himself to mankind. He continues to reveal Himself today in many ways: for example, through Scripture, through the gifts of the Holy Spirit and through the Holy Spirit's inner witness in our lives.

📖 *Read: Psalm 32:8, Psalm 119:133, 1 Kings 19:12, Ezekiel 43:2, Nehemiah 9:20,Luke 12:12, John 14: 26, 1 Corinthians 2:13.*

❓ **Question**: What do the following passages tell us about God that could not be known without special communication or 'special revelation'?
- John 3:16
- Exodus 20:17
- Luke 12:6-7
- Matthew 25:31-46
- Psalm 138:8
- 1 John 1:9
- Hebrews 13:4
- Song of Songs 4:1-16
- Ephesians 5:1-3

? **Question**: Which passages refer to His special knowledge, to His loving care, to His graciousness, to immorality, to the inward nature of sin?

? **Question**: Could we have known these things about God unless the Bible said so?

### GOD REVEALS HIMSELF THROUGH A LIBRARY OF BOOKS – THE BIBLE!

Many of the things God spoke to individuals He caused to be written down, together with the things God did for them, and these writings were kept by people who loved God and made eventually into the book we call the Bible. This is actually a collection of books written by many different people over a period of over a thousand years. God Himself made sure that what was written was exactly what He wanted – nothing more or less.

Most of what we call the 'Old Testament' was written in Hebrew, with small portions in Aramaic, and the 'New Testament' in Greek. Some translations into English are more useful or appropriate than others. It is sometimes useful to compare different versions.

God spoke many times in Old Testament days but the words were not always recorded. What has been written down has value *not only for the time it was given, but for today*.

📖 *Read: 2 Timothy 3:14-17 ('inspired' here means literally 'God-breathed').*

? **Question**: Name four specific objectives of Scripture.

📖 *Read: 2 Peter 1:20-21. Not that Scripture is not man's idea about God, but it is God's revelation to us!*

? **Question**: Who does the apostle Peter say is the author of Scripture?

? **Question**: In addition to Scripture's own claim to authority, for what reasons would you personally place confidence in its truth/accuracy?

? **Question**: Try and answer Yes or No to the following:

1. Our conscience agrees with Scripture about right and wrong.

2. The creation around us gives enough evidence of God to make us need more.

3. The Scriptures are accurate in what we can learn from history about the true nature of man. This gives us confidence to trust the 'promises for today and tomorrow' that are in the Bible.

4. Other philosophies tend to contradict each other and in the end don't really meet human need.

5. The consistent way the writers of Scripture speak from God's perspective testifies to its Divine origin.

The 'special revelation' of God in Scripture consists of two main sections – the 'Old Testament' and the 'New Testament'. With the exception of Luke (a medical doctor who wrote one of the gospels and Acts) all the authors were Jewish.

The Old Testament writings contain a lot of ancient history – but history as seen through God's eyes. They contain the laws which God gave through Moses. They contain songs of worship and poetic writings. And they contain the words God spoke through the prophets – men who were inspired by God to remind or to teach the people what He had previously said, and to prepare them for the future – especially for the time when God would reveal Himself in person in a more wonderful way than ever before, or since! The New Testament has not replaced or rendered obsolete the Old Testament. Rather it has added to it. The New has fulfilled the Old Testament. All the promises (covenants) God made in the Old Testament, because of His very nature, He has fulfilled or He must fulfil. God cannot break a promise He has made!

## JESUS CHRIST IS THE FULL AND FINAL REVELATION OF GOD TO MAN – HE IS BOTH FULLY GOD AND HE IS FULLY MAN

📖　*Read: Hebrews 1:1-3.*

These words describe a development or unfolding of revelation, culminating in the God-man, Jesus Christ. The New Testament is a record of His life and work together with God's own interpretation of what that means for us. The Old Testament was accurate and sufficient for its purpose in the days before Jesus. The New Testament brings clarity and completeness to that revelation. For us today, the Old Testament is a little bit like a picture out of focus but slowly becoming more clear. The New Testament is by comparison like a picture fully in focus, but also in 3-D, allowing a clear picture of God's plans for building a new relationship with His human creation. The Old Testament points forward to the promised Messiah, the Lord

37

Jesus, and the New Testament says, 'Here He is.' Both Old and new Testaments tell us He will come again a second time.

The whole of the Bible, correctly understood, is designed to direct our attention to the Son of God who became man. In the Bible, and in Jesus Christ, God has revealed to us all that we need to know about Himself and ourselves: where we came from, why we are here and where we are going.

📖 *Read: John 1:1-18.*

In John 1:1-3 we read of the 'Word of God'. In verse 14, we have the amazing statement that 'the Word (of God) became flesh and lived among us'. This is yet another way of saying that Jesus is the eternal revelation (word) of God, who was with God active in creation, and who 'became human', so revealing God to us more fully.

To sum up what we have covered so far in this study of the nature of God: there are FIVE areas in which God is fundamentally different from us. They are:

– God is 'spiritual'
– God is 'omnipotent'
– God is 'omniscient'
– God is 'omnipresent'
– God is 'eternal'.

❓ **Question**: what do each of these five words above mean? Try and write in 'everyday English' a short definition of each. Write the definition in a way a non-Christian friend, neighbour or work colleague could understand.

It may be useful to use a good dictionary to help you with this task!

# Week 3:
# THE NATURE OF THE GOD
# WE WORSHIP

## GROUP WORK SECTION

This week will consist of a brief discussion on how each member 'got on' with their individual tasks. They were:

1. Prayer/fasting

2. The memory verse (John 16:33)

3. Individual Bible study

After this your study leader will then go through last week's 'individual study' entitled 'How do we know what God is like?' He or she will ask each to discuss the answers they have given and the conclusions reached. This will involve general discussion as the review proceeds.

The leader will then outline the individual tasks for next week. They are:

1. Individual Bible study that will help you to develop further your understanding of what the Bible tells us of what God is like. Again work through the study and be ready to share your answers and conclusions next week.

2. Individual prayer target. Try and spend at least 20-30 minutes each day in prayer. Develop a suitable structure for your prayer list. Again try and fast for one day before the next group meeting. Perhaps fast over a specific issue or prayer request.

3. Memorise a new verse of Scripture: 1 Corinthians 3:16

## INDIVIDUAL WORK SECTION

This section is for individual study. Your conclusions, queries, questions and answers will be discussed at the next group meeting, as will those of other group members.

In Weeks 1 and 2, we investigated the fact that we need God to show us what He is really like. Guesswork, imagination and careful thinking even by the most able will not give us a true picture of God.

We have considered how God has revealed Himself to man, through the world He has made, through the Bible, God's written Word: especially as the written Word reveals the Living Word – the Lord Jesus Christ.

What we are going to do next is to discover what we can about God the intelligent creative being, His personality and character so that we will know the kind of God we are following and worshipping. Knowing *about* Him is not the same thing as knowing Him *personally*. The only way to know Him personally is to be introduced (or to introduce oneself) to Him and then to spend time with Him. If we do know Him already, further insights will help us to appreciate our Father in heaven more. If we don't know Him yet, learning about Him will create a desire to get to know Him and give a sense of excitement in anticipation of meeting such a glorious, mysterious, powerful, awesome, loving and wise Being.

## SO WHAT IS THE GOD WE WORSHIP REALLY LIKE ?

We can divide what God is like into two halves – His personality (what it is that makes Him God, and therefore very different) and His character (aspects of Him that can be imparted to us, the ways in which He wants us to be like Him).

41

Take for example His *personality*; He is one-in-three (a Trinity). He is eternal. We are neither! Whereas examples of His *character* are His honesty and gentleness, things He can impart to us.

We must keep reminding ourselves just how much greater than man God is. It is difficult to try and comprehend the size, personality, character and love of God. As a consequence, man often tries to invent gods he can understand. Or he tries to make the God of the Bible and Christianity small enough and limited enough to understand. Often modern 'scientific/ technological' man feels more comfortable with a god he can measure with 'a yardstick' (explaining away bits he does not comprehend such as miracles, the bodily resurrection of Jesus, the divinity of Jesus and places such as heaven and hell). Keep reminding yourself of the picture of the ant trying to understand the gardener (1 Kings 8:27).

The Bible tells us that God is so big, so powerful, so awesome that if in our present bodies we saw God face to face we would probably die. Our physical human form could not cope with it: perhaps a little like connecting a 12 V bulb to a 240 V supply, a dangerous act that would burn out the 12 V bulb almost instantaneously! Don't despair however, God understands all of this; remember He created us and wants a very close and loving relationship with His creation – us! So that this is possible, He has created a way for us to have a wonderful, close, loving relationship with Him the perfect Father. 'Perfect' is a concept that may be hard for those whose relationship with their human father is or was not good.

So with confidence that we are only doing what God intends us to do, let us look at God's revelation of Himself to us and try to discover what the God we worship is really like! First, let us deal with the triune (three-in-one) nature of God.

## *THE GOD WE WORSHIP IS THREE QUITE SEPARATE BEINGS TOGETHER IN ONE UNITED BEING*

The God we worship, is three Persons in one – one God but three Persons. A difficult concept to understand! The only way of approaching this is to look at what is written in the Bible. That is, to read how God Himself has explained it! First we will deal with the oneness, the uniqueness of God.

### GOD IS ONE BEING

📖 *Read: Deuteronomy 6:4.*

The law was given by God to Moses originally on Mount Sinai, and then repeated nearly 40 years later by Moses as the Israelites were on the point of entering the promised land. In Deuteronomy 5:1-22 (and previously in Exodus 20:1-21) we have the 'Ten Commandments'. Some of the 'ten' deal with our relationship with God and others with the way we behave to and with each other.

❓ **Question**: Which commandments are especially significant in the light of Deuteronomy 6:4 – 'The Lord your God is One'?

📖 *Read: 2 Samuel 7:22.*

❓ **Question**: What is the significant clause in this verse of praise by David in relation to the oneness of God?

43

&#x1F4D6;   *Read: Isaiah 43:8-13.*

God is challenging all people to acknowledge His uniqueness. Try to put verses 10 and 11 into your own words. It is made very clear in Is. 44:6 and elsewhere. God is making it quite clear that He has no equal, will not tolerate other gods being worshipped. He is leaving no room for doubt, that He alone is the one true God! In Mark 12: 28-34 Jesus quotes the passage in Deuteronomy. This endorses the correctness of the words given to Moses, and shows us that Jesus was fully aware of and utterly committed to the concept of the oneness of God Himself.

## GOD IS THREE SEPARATE BEINGS

There is good evidence for the distinctiveness of the persons within the Godhead. A number of verses link the three 'Persons of the Trinity' together and give a clue about their relationship, and show that each has His own name and role.

&#x1F4D6;   *Read and compare Matt. 28: 18-20 with 2 Corinthians 13:14.*

Note that the same words are not always used. Christians often refer to the 1st, 2nd and 3rd persons of the Trinity. Now fill in the following chart – watch the order carefully!

|  | 1st person | 2nd person | 3rd person |
|---|---|---|---|
| Matt. 28:19 |  |  |  |
| 2 Corinthians 13:14 |  |  |  |

The verses above do not actually spell out that each of the three persons is God, so we need to consider passages that do state this.

Below is one example for each – underline the correct answer.

- 1 Corinthians 8:6. Who is directly affirmed to be God in this verse? Father/Son/Holy Spirit

- John 20:24-29. Who is directly affirmed to be God in v.28? Father/Son/Holy Spirit

- 1 Cor. 3:16-17. Who is directly affirmed to be God in these verses? Father/Son/Holy Spirit

## GOD IS THREE SEPARATE BEINGS

In this, we have established that there is one God, but also that three distinct Beings or Persons are all called that one God. For human logic this concept is difficult to understand. We must not forget in all of this that the immensity of God is far beyond our understanding. To attempt to 'cut Him down' to a size that we can understand, would not be a true understanding of God (remember the ant and the gardener).

📖 *Read: Is. 45:20-23 and Philippians 2:5-11.*

❓ **Question**: Compare and contrast carefully the last half of Is. 45:23 with Phil. 2:10-11. Who is being spoken of in each case? Is it clear that Jehovah – the God of Israel – is being identified totally with Jesus Christ of Nazareth?

The last part of Philippians 2:11 says that this exaltation of Jesus is 'to the glory of God the Father' – but what does God say in Isaiah 42:8? What is said of God the Father is also said of God the Son! Jesus is clearly God! The identical point is made when we compare what the apostle John says in 12:37-41 with Isaiah 6:1-3.

45

📖 *Read: John 14:15-26.*

Jesus revealed many profound truths in the days just before His death. This passage is a profound illustration of the role and relationship within the three-in-one Being that we call God (Father, Son, Holy Spirit). It describes how the Father will react if we love the Son, how the Father will react when the Son returns to Him, and how the Father will care for us whilst the Son is with Him, by sending the third Being/Person of the triune God – the Holy Spirit, as a Counsellor to dwell in us, to teach us, guide us, strengthen us and give us victory through the shed blood of Jesus, against all forces that oppose God and therefore us. The Spirit is to be our link to the Father via the Son.

In verse 16 Jesus promises to pray to the Father so that He (the Father) will send to the disciples (and us) another Helper (Counsellor, Encourager, Advocate, Comforter), who will then remain with believers forever. In verse 17 He makes it clear that this 'other Helper' is the Holy Spirit (here called the Spirit of Truth). Jesus says, ' *You already know Him – because He is with you – and will then be in you'*. As He speaks, Jesus is with the disciples, but The Holy Spirit will soon be in them – once Jesus has returned to the Father. The Holy Spirit, whom He refers to again at the end of Chapter 15 (verses 26 and 27), as being sent by Him but from the Father, will then bear witness to Jesus. This is further explained in Chapter 16:13-15 where Jesus says that the Spirit will glorify Him. In Chapter 16:7 Jesus says that they will be better off when He has gone and the Spirit has come! But then back in Chapter 14:18 Jesus says that He will come to them! Jesus and the Spirit are separate, but inseparable! Chapter 14:20-26 emphasises further the mystery of the oneness in the Godhead. Be encouraged by the help promised in understanding all of this and get excited by verse 26! Note that in verse 26 Jesus talks about the Holy Spirit as a *person*, not as a mysterious force, or some kind of energy or mystic New Age power. The New Living Translation (NLT) translates it as: *'He will teach you everything and will remind you of everything I myself have told you.'* It seems clear to *God (Jesus)*, that another equal being *God (the Holy Spirit)* will take over the role of that part of the triune God that is in direct communication with man.

So to return to an earlier thought, this is how *God (The Father)* has chosen to communicate with us through *God (Jesus)* who is fully man and fully God; and while we are here on earth in this life we are helped by 'the Enabler ' *God (The Holy Spirit)* who dwells in us.

? **Questions**:

1. Who is with the disciples in the discourse in John Chapters 14-16?

2. Who is going to be in them?

3. Who sends the 'other helper'?

In the passage in John we see primarily the Son and the Spirit identified. We have seen how the Father and Son are one; now we will look at how in a remarkable way the Father and the Spirit are identified, by ascribing to each of them exactly the same work!

📖 *Read: Luke 10:21-24 and 1 Corinthians 2:10-12.*

? **Question**: Who is revealing the hidden things?

*THE FATHER AND THE SON ARE ONE BEING*
*THE SON AND THE SPIRIT ARE ONE BEING*
*THE FATHER AND THE SPIRIT ARE ONE BEING*

47

Therefore:

*GOD THE FATHER, GOD THE SON AND GOD THE HOLY SPIRIT ARE **ONE** BEING!*

But each maintains His own individuality!

There are many places in Scripture where the individual identity of each person of the Trinity is clear. We will look at one in particular which illustrates their relationship. Read carefully Matthew 3:13-17. Verses 16 and 17 describe Jesus the Son of God being baptised, the Spirit of God comes upon Him like a dove, and the Father expresses His pleasure and satisfaction by speaking from Heaven! You can see illustrated in these verses total harmony, but there is also separate identity.

So to sum up what the Bible is saying:

The Father is God; the Son is God; the Spirit is God, but the Father is not the Son, the Son is not the Spirit, and the Spirit is not the Father. However it is clear that there is total integration between the three at a level that is totally incomprehensible to mankind!

*ONE GOD BUT THREE INDIVIDUAL PERSONS*

A very deep truth – as human beings we cannot expect to understand the nature of God, the creator of the universe!

## GOD IS UNIQUE AND MYSTERIOUS

The nature of the relationships within the Godhead is probably going to remain to some extent a mystery. What we do know is revealed for our benefit, and is necessary for us to know it. How else could we conceive of the love of God in dying for us if Jesus is not God? How else could we be convinced of the power within us to make us Christ-like if the Holy Spirit is not God? These things are vitally important for us to know, but they are not everything. God not only has a three-fold existence but He has a unique personality. He is not like us in this either!

God is not confined by space or time; thus He is infinitely large and everywhere at the same time! Travel is a big thing for humans – but God does not need to go from place to place. He is everywhere! He is what is called omnipresent.

Solomon the temple-builder understood this, and His reaction to the visible presence of God in the new temple at Jerusalem shows it. (See 1 Kings 8:27). God is not only here but at the far end of the universe – wherever that is!

### ？ **Questions**:

1. How would you explain this to a friend? David the Psalm-writer states that even if he wanted to get away from God it would be completely impossible.

*Read Psalm 139:7-12. Jeremiah the prophet, speaking as God's mouthpiece, puts it very plainly. Read Jeremiah 23:22-23. He brings together Solomon's thought of God's omnipresence with David's sense of not being able to escape from him!*

2. In what way do the passages on the omnipresence of God affect us?

3. Do you find such a concept exciting or do you find it threatening? Why? In some ways this doctrine convicts; in other ways it comforts.

4. How does it affect the way I worship?

5. How does it affect the way I pray?

6. How does it affect the way I behave in secret?

7. How does it affect my attitude to loneliness?

## GOD IS EVERYWHERE – NOT BOUND BY SPACE OR TIME !

Not only is God everywhere at the same time, because He is God, He is also an absolute ruler with absolute power. He is in charge – of everything. He has no serious rivals. Satan, a self-declared rival, is really a rebellious ex-senior angel, destined for destruction. About one third of all angels rebelled against God – bad or fallen angels.

📖 *Read: Revelation 12:9. No earthly ruler dare defy God – except in the arrogance of ignorance like Herod in Acts 12:21-23! Sometimes God's retribution does not appear immediate to us – but it is always sure!*

## HE IS THE ABSOLUTE RULER AND HAS ABSOLUTE POWER

❓ **Question**: Psalm 115:3 says: *'He does whatever pleases Him!'* Think about those words.

50

How do you react:

– with fear?

– with anger?

– with joy and peace?

Why do you think you react to this in the way you do?

However we may react to it the absoluteness of God remains. This aspect of God's nature is called omnipotence. What we should remember is the size, strength and completeness of God's love for each of us, no matter who we are or what we have done!

📖 *Read: Jeremiah 31:3; John 3:16; Romans 5:8 and 1 John 3:1. What is clear is that we should not fear this absolute ruler with His absolute power!*

Jeremiah the prophet drew comfort from His knowledge of God's Sovereignty in creation. If God made the whole universe out of nothing, then He can do anything – and Jeremiah is not going to give God a problem whatever he prays! This thought is repeated by Jesus.

📖 *Read: Matt. 19:26. Then look up the magnificent passage in Isaiah (Chapter 40) about the majesty and power of God. Read the whole chapter (again). Think about it carefully – dwell on it.*

Isaiah 40 can be analysed under three main themes:

1. God's greatness.

2. Man's smallness.

3. The benefits we little humans may have through trusting Him.

？ **Question**: Break down Isaiah 40 into sections, as follows, and then allocate each section to one of the above headings: Verses 1-2, 3-5, 6-8, 9-11, 12-14, 18, 19-20, 21-22, 22-24, 25-26 and 27-31.

The words of a well-known chorus are appropriate here:

> *Our Lord God, thou hast made the heavens and the earth by thy great power!*
>
> *Our Lord God, thou hast made the heavens and the earth by thy outstretched hand!*
>
> *Nothing is too difficult for thee ...*
>
> *Nothing is too difficult for thee ...*

## LET US BUILD ON THE STUDY SO FAR

God is everywhere in the universe He created; He knows everything about the universe He created; as a result He literally knows and understands everything! This is a difficult concept for modern man to grasp. God also has immense wisdom and together with His great love (which we have already discussed), He is completely wise in all He does.

King David understood this and applied it in a very personal way (see Psalm 139:1-6). God's acceptance of us is not based on His ignorance of us! Simply, He knows all, even the very worst about us, but still loves us. It is pointless pretending with God! We cannot hide from him, we cannot deceive Him in any way! If we try, all we do is deceive ourselves! Paul (in Romans 11:33) finds the wisdom of God really exciting; it certainly puts human wisdom in its place and it becomes for him a cause of spontaneous praise (v.36).

Not only does God know the past and the present but He knows the future also. He can predict events and their outcome. Compare Isaiah 53 with the gospel records of Christ's death and Paul's interpretation of it. Just read the Isaiah passage and see how it fits with what you already know of the death of Christ.

God's knowledge and power together enable Him to overrule all the malicious intentions of Satan and of wicked men so that everything works out in the end the way He intends. This can be seen for example in connection with the crucifixion.

📖 *Read: Acts 2:22-24 and Acts 4:27-28. One is part of a sermon, the other is part of a prayer, but they both show the confidence God's people had in His ability to govern the world with wisdom and power – and to turn what might have seemed to be the world's greatest disaster into its greatest blessing!*

In comparison with that of God, man's wisdom in relative terms is worth little. Usually in trying to be wise, man starts in the wrong place – *with himself* and with his own understanding!

📖 *Read: Psalm 111: 10.*

As was mentioned earlier, God invented time but He Himself lives outside of time; in the same way He is not constrained by physical space. He is eternal as well as omnipresent. That is He had no beginning and will have no end! Again for humans where everything we know or experience has a beginning and an end, this concept is difficult to imagine: another important difference between God and us that we need to grasp!

God is also the same, yesterday, today and in the future – throughout the duration of eternity past God has not changed and in the depths of future eternity God will not change. He is constant, unchanging.

📖 *Read: Psalm 102:25-28. Note the contrast between the limited timescale of the created Universe (all that we know) compared to the eternal 'unchangeableness' of God! This is quoted in full in Hebrews 1:10-12. Read and compare the two passages and their context.*

📖 *Read: Malachi 3:6.*

The last of the Old Testament prophets, Malachi, derives comfort for God's people from this doctrine. Similarly James encourages us to rely on the 'unchangeableness' of God in James 1:17.

❓ **Question**: What comfort do you derive from the eternal unchanging nature of God?

📖 *Read: Psalm 102:27; Hebrews 13:8; Psalm 18:30-32 and Psalm 28.*

## GOD IS HERE FOR EVER, UNCHANGING AND UTTERLY RELIABLE

Faced with the God we have been exploring, vast, powerful, awesome, majestic and mysterious, we should be convinced of the frailty of man. Again, remember the ant and the gardener analogy? As unpalatable as it may be to modern knowledgeable man – able to build aircraft, computers and develop wonder medical drugs – his achievements measured against those of God, are (at the most charitable) – trivial! Before such a God we are as Isaiah says, like 'grasshoppers' or 'small drops in a bucket'. How ridiculous for us to challenge Him, defy Him, rebel against Him, or blaspheme His name! He has got us weighed, knows our every thought, and could crush us out of existence by merely thinking about it!

A task to conclude this section: *During your next prayer time humble yourself before the creator of the universe, the one true God, through the name of Jesus, seek forgiveness for man's arrogance and praise and thank God for who He is.*

## SUMMING UP THIS SECTION

It is futile and arrogant to try and capture God in an idol. Isaiah graphically describes this in Chapter 44 verses 9 to 20. Verses 16 and 17 sum it up for its folly! Yet Paul, in Romans 1:18-25, has to expose the stupidity of those who suppress the truth of their creator God and substitute idols. Time and time again, we hear 'mother nature' or the 'theory of evolution' made into a substitute creator in countless beautifully filmed TV documentaries. Refer to the earlier section, where we discussed this. Modern humanist man finds it difficult and sometimes even offensive to accept the reality of a creator God who is way beyond their understanding. At its most charitable it goes against their training, but perhaps for some it is a matter of pride or a misunderstanding about what the Christian God is all about or perhaps from a bad experience. So they find substitutes, perhaps a crude carving or a sophisticated but essentially man-made theory. But as we have already said, God does not change; He is still there no matter how hard man tries to ignore Him.

There are other aspects of God's nature which we will explore in the next section that contrast wonderfully with the power and the enormity of God! – aspects that show Him to be a loving Father, concerned about every detail of life that concerns us!

# Week 4:
# A LOVING CARING GOD?

## GROUP WORK SECTION

This week will consist of a brief discussion on how each member 'got on' with their individual tasks. They were:

1. Prayer/fasting

2. The memory verse (1 Corinthians 3:16)

3. Individual Bible study

After this your study leader will then go through last week's 'individual study' entitled 'The nature of the God we worship'. He will ask each to discuss the answers they have given and the conclusions reached. This will involve general discussion as the review proceeds.

The leader will then outline the individual tasks for next week. They are:

1. Individual Bible study that will help you to develop further your understanding of what the Bible tells us of what God is like. Again work through the study and be ready to share your answers and conclusions next week.

2. Individual prayer target. Try and spend at least 20-30 minutes each day in prayer. Develop a suitable structure for your prayer list. Again try and fast for one day before the next group meeting. Perhaps fast over a specific issue or prayer request.

3. Memorise a new verse of Scripture: 1 Peter 5:7.

## INDIVIDUAL STUDY

This section is for individual study. Your conclusions, queries, questions and answers will be discussed at the next group meeting, as will those of other group members.

The different aspects of the nature of a creating God that we have considered so far all emphasise how utterly different He is from all created beings and how different He is from us! When Moses asked God who He was and what was His name (Exodus 3:13-15) God replied, 'I AM' or 'I AM who I AM'. Not too helpful one might say – but it is expressing the inexpressible and describing the incomprehensible. He alone is self-sufficient, self-existent, the ground of all being, the source of all life. How do you put that into human ideas and words?

But in fact there are many other things we can learn about God, things that impinge more directly on us!

God's desire is to communicate with us – but to do more than impart information. His purpose is that within the limits of our finite existence we should share as much of His nature as possible, and have a relationship forever based on His grace and His love! Such a desire by God takes our individual salvation out of the realm of simply sinners being forgiven, as important as that is: it lifts the created into a dynamic relationship of love – with the creator!

*GOD WANTS US TO BE LIKE HIM IN SOME*
*IMPORTANT WAYS*

The God who is outside of time, who had no beginning and has no end, who is not bound by physical space or distance, became mortal (human) so as to bring us into the centre of His purposes for the future. How He does this we will look at later.

📖 *Read: Exodus 34:1-9.*

Moses had other revelations of God at various times. After the sad story of the golden calf, and the replacement of the original broken stone tablets with the Ten Commandments written on them, the Lord 'passed before Moses'. He proclaimed Himself as 'The Lord God, merciful and gracious, long suffering, abounding in goodness and truth, keeping mercy, forgiving iniquity, transgression and sin, but punishing those who fully deserve it, and treating all of the human race as responsible beings who must bear the consequences of their actions.'

This involves a whole new set of revelations about God – issues that govern the way He relates to us. Here God is setting the ground rules for the communication between Himself and man. Not that He wants to be difficult or a 'spoilsport', but because of His nature, His abhorrence of sin and His desire to see us more like him. When His laws are broken therefore, His communication relationship with us is impossible. Thus rebellious sinners have to be removed from His presence.

*GOD IS UTTERLY HOLY – HE THEREFORE CANNOT TOLERATE SIN OF ANY KIND!*

When we say 'God is Holy' what do we mean? What is a holy person? Is he or she strict, priggish, quaint, old-fashioned? Is he or she a spoilsport, dour, negative, disliking fun and laughter? Someone perhaps who wants to impose strict harsh rules on others, to govern every aspect of life? God's holiness has two aspects – His 'majestic holiness' and His 'moral holiness'.

📖 *Read: Exodus 15:11 and Is. 6:1-5.*

God is awesome, wonderful, different, indeed frightening (see also Hebrews 12:18-29). His holiness provoked a reaction in Moses and Isaiah and there is a similar response by Peter to Jesus Christ in Luke 5:5-10. It was this same 'majestic holiness' that brought Paul to the ground on the Damascus Road and caused John to collapse on Patmos. Overwhelmed with awe, people were stunned into immobility and silence. Unless experienced (and today it is being experienced by increasing numbers of Christians) it is a concept difficult to describe. The human is unable to cope with the size, power and beauty of the experience. You can have just a small experience of this when you look down for the first time into, say, the Grand Canyon in Colorado USA. It is when the experience is so big, that human senses cannot cope, are overloaded and in effect have 'systems failure'! This majestic holiness of God can be understood a little by looking at those who have experienced it for themselves.

❓ **Question**: Have you experienced in a small way something of the holiness and majesty of God? YES/NO If so, in what sort of context have you experienced it e.g. during worship, private prayer, as a vision, or some other experience? Describe in your own words a proper response to the 'majestic holiness' of God.

The other awesome aspect of God's holiness is His absolute moral purity – His total abhorrence of sin. He made the rules – He keeps them perfectly! The prophets were all very much aware of this. In Daniel's prayer (Daniel 9:1-19), and in Habakkuk's confusion as he cries out to God (Habakkuk 1:13).

61

The New Testament clearly describes God's holiness.

📖 *Read: 1 Peter 1:13-16.*

❓ **Question**: Why is it so important for us to live a holy life?

## A PRAYER

Not an easy one for many to pray until you get to know the Father and you are able to trust Him. Try praying it:

> *O Lord, you are righteous and your decisions are fair. Your decrees are perfect; they are entirely worthy of our trust.*

### GOD KEEPS ALL HIS OWN RULES!

Righteousness and justice are closely linked. Righteousness is personal behaviour that is totally honest and fair. Justice is the administration of society in such a way that it strongly encourages personal honesty and fairness. A righteous person is someone who is able to live in contact with others but without any moral blemishes or failures (sin) at all. Perhaps impossible for humans but it is God's own standard. This is what He is like: *'Entirely worthy of our trust'*.

The best form of government so far created by mankind is where *justice* is enforced by society through laws that are created by democratically elected representatives. This provides laws which *all* in society are subject to. This is usually called the 'rule of law' and the best we have. God's *justice* comes through His righteousness. It is different; but mankind can experience a little of God's righteousness and therefore His concept of justice, from deep inner conviction through the work of The Holy Spirit and from time spent with God in prayer and worship.

Sometimes however, human justice is not fair; rules can be made by even democratically elected men and women seeking personal power, wealth or other desires such as worldly views of 'correctness' or populist pressures. Also, laws can be misapplied or waived. God is however always fair in His dealings with us. Many of the authors who wrote parts of the Bible understood this. One expressed feelings of happiness at the completeness of God's justice and expressed it in Psalm 119:137-138. In Isaiah 3:10-11 we are told of God's justice, and in Romans 6:5-6, Paul emphasises God's justice in terms of rewards and punishments. God is just and righteous, all the injustices of this present life will therefore be set right in the life that is to come. Jesus made references to this.

📖 *Read: Matthew. 5:11-12, 25:31-46, Luke 16:19-31.*

❓ **Questions**:

1. Read Luke 16 verse 25 again – what does it mean? How would you explain God's point of view to a friend?

2. Can we expect to receive the sort of justice that the Bible is talking about in this life?

3. Should we aim for justice in this life, in particular for others, wherever possible?

4. What is our guarantee that justice will finally be done?

It has been said that *'political leaders of modern society, in their attempt to be populist and their desire to be on good terms with vocal single-issue pressure groups, adopt issues perceived to win them "votes"'*. One such and perhaps just popular concern adopted by politicians, is the reduction of crime, *'as every citizen has the right to live in a crime free society'*. To do all of this, politicians in several democratic countries have introduced laws which go against traditional biblical principles. Making certain activities lawful may reduce crime in the short term, but what will be the long-term effect for both society and the individual of breaking God's law?

**?**   **Question**: If the laws of society are modelled on God's law, will this infringe on personal freedom?

📖   *Read: Daniel 4:31, Hebrews 13:17, John 19:11, Romans 13: 1-4 and 1 Peter 2:17*

### IF GOD REALLY IS 'ENTIRELY WORTHY OF OUR TRUST' WHAT DOES ALL THIS MEAN?

The holiness, righteousness and justice of God are in one sense comfort on their own. If that was the full nature of God – morally strict, remote, determined to dispel punishment, harsh on those who do not obey His 'impossible' code to the letter – then for each of us, the future looks terrifying! But don't get too worried there is real hope.

📖   *Read: John 8: 3-11.*

As we are all too well aware, none of us are free of 'skeletons in the cupboard'. We have all done wrong at some point and fallen far short of keeping God's laws to the letter. It is interesting that as we get older we become more aware of this: see John 8:1-11 (in particular verse 9). Guilt is something we instinctively feel in God's presence. In Exodus 19, and 20: 18-21, the people experience terror in the presence of God the lawgiver.

Job, in spite of His apparent righteousness, felt only guilt and shame before God.

📖 *Read: Job12:1-4. Contrast and compare with Job 40:3-5, and 42:2-6.*

❓ **Question**: *'If we have never experienced personal sinfulness and a sense of "smallness" before God, we have never understood what God is really like.'* Do you agree with this statement? Think about and then describe your reaction.

## SO WHAT THEN IS GOD REALLY LIKE – THE FULL PICTURE?

An understanding of the 'holiness and righteousness' aspect of God's complex character, enables us to really appreciate both His loving kindness and His gracious mercy when He reveals them to us.

*OUR GOD IS ALSO A GOOD GOD*

The origin of the word 'goodness' is 'everything that comes from God', thus what radiates from God. Heat from a fire on a cold evening or light from a spotlight on a dark night, is good. But the goodness of God takes many forms, see Psalm 34:8, where David expresses His experiences of God.

📖 *Read: Psalm 145. This is another of David's Psalms of praise. He describes God's benevolence, that is His loving desire to care for His creation, as a loving parent would for a young helpless, vulnerable child.*

But God's love and care goes far beyond that of the most loving perfect parent possible. In verse 9, David says that God literally 'showers compassion on all His creation'. Look at verse 14, 'God helps the fallen and lifts up those bent beneath their (heavy) load'. (NLT) Read the story of King David in full, he was not writing 'romantic' poetry here: rather he was speaking from real tough personal experiences of life and his dealings with God. This is the goodness of God, He cares about every detail of each of us!

*OUR GOD **IS** LOVE – THAT IS LOVE IN ITS MOST PURE AND WONDERFUL FORM!*

Today the word *love* is most often used with a romantic meaning (they fell in *love*) or a sexual meaning (they made *love*). In addition, tabloid newspapers use it to sensationalise adultery and eroticism (married footballer has secret love nest). At its most basic, the word *love* can be used for a couple who 'made love' after a casual meeting at say a holiday resort night club, where they just fancied each other: a relationship so casual that whilst they were 'making love' they knew almost nothing about each other having perhaps met for the first time less than two hours earlier, possibly not knowing, or wanting to know, each other's name! This legacy from the use of the word *love* by the film and music industry in particular, which has affected us all in modern society, needs correcting if we are to begin to grasp what the concept of *love* means to God!

The Bible identifies four different kinds of love in the Greek:

1. *Agape love* – a universal love; a love of the will that operates when it is neither attracted nor reciprocated. It is a sacrificial unselfish love.

2. *Philia love* – a selective love, emotional and dependent on the loveable qualities it sees in its object.

3. *Eros love* – the desire to get and possess; egocentric love but can often be of the highest kind and can often be very deep love.

4. *Storge love* – family or tribal love.

In our common every day Christian usage, we see agape love as God loving all humanity, each of us as we are, simply because He wants to! We usually translate philial love as brotherly love, and eros love as romantic or erotic love. In 1 John 4:10-11, the Bible says:

> *...this is real love. It is not that we loved God, but that He loved us and sent His son as a sacrifice to take away our sins ...Dear friends, since God loved us that much, we surely ought to love each other! (NLT)*

### ？ **Questions**:

1. What kinds of love does John express here?

2. How should we react to this verse?

3. What very practical steps can we take?

The 1 John 4 passage above encapsulates the theme of the traditional Christian understanding of God's love. It has four facets:

1. It is God-centred, because the source of genuine love, the highest form of love, lies in God's love for us His creation and how He has expressed it. See: 1 John 4:8 and 16(b).

2. It is an expression of God's love centred on Jesus Christ, in that Jesus is the focal point of God's love. See: Mark 1:11, Mark 9:7.

3. It is active and self-sacrificial, expressed ultimately in the death of Jesus on the cross. See: John 3:16, Galatians 2:20 and Romans 5:5.

4. It demands a response, an acceptance from those who want to receive God's expressed love. See: John 8:42, 2 Corinthians 5:14, Galatians 5:6 and 1 Timothy 1:14. Also: Hebrews 6:10, Matthew 25:34-40 and 1 John 4:20.

**Question**: How does each of these four facets of God's love affect situations and relationships that you will face in your life this week? Identify four key situations and try and see how God's love relates to them.

Many Christian bookshops currently have a number of books containing compilations of 'comforting' words of Scripture for times of difficulty, times of despair, times of grief etc.; also books of encouragement with words of Scripture for times of weakness or seemingly endless toil. Some verge on the sentimental and are often 'sloppy' when describing God's love. The verses are often supported by 'emotion-manipulating' photographs, drawings and words. There is no doubt that some do really find such things helpful, but it is only showing one (unbalanced) view of God. There is also a need for books that denounce sin, challenging the spiritually inept and 'laying it on the line' with the comfortable lukewarm. The Bible describes itself (the word of God) as a 'two-edged sword'. Not a comfortable picture, as a genuine encounter can be very spiritually challenging and often unsettling! In Scripture God regularly has some harsh words to say to His people when they are settling for less than the target He has set for them. God's word can be tough in its demands of us, if it were not for Jesus. Although it is often Jesus who makes the tough challenges; the one who *'knows our every weakness, but loves us just the same'*, also knows how hard it can be being a human. If Jesus asks us to go further or do more, it is because He is waiting there at the destination for us having 'prepared a place'. If Jesus reminds us of our sins, it is because He is waiting for us and wants to forgive us before 'moving on together'.

## ?  Questions:

1. How should we approach God's throne of grace in worship and prayer to receive His mercy and His help?

2. For the following categories of people, what alternative word or words would you use in John 3:16? *'For God so loved the world that He gave His only Son so that everyone who believes in Him will not perish but have eternal life.'* (NLT)

- For a child under eight.

- For a work colleague who beneath the surface is lonely and hurt by life.

- For a neighbour struggling alone with unruly children and little money.

- For an elderly person in failing health.

To return again to some beautiful but powerful verses: in 1 John 4:10 it says: *'...this is real love. It is not that we loved God, but that He loved us and sent His son as a sacrifice to take away* [pay the penalty for, take the 'rap' for] *our sins.'* Compare this with the verse in John 3:16. In both we see God's act of SELF-sacrifice.

God sometimes expresses His love emotionally, in Jesus weeping over the death of Lazarus or in the intense pain when He anticipated His sufferings in Gethsemane (Luke 22:44); but God's love is expressed in His determination to do good to us whatever it costs Him. It is the commitment to our best interests that will take Him to self-sacrifice. Note how the Father sent the Son, but the Son came willingly. They are one in their LOVE for us!

## OUR GOD IS LOVE – PURE LOVE

This love expresses itself in both mercy and in forgiveness (Romans 5:8). His mercy (willingness to forgive) has over-ruled His strict justice – as far as we are concerned – but His justice has been satisfied (we will deal with this in a later week). He did not have to forgive us – but He did and that is the most important issue! God takes no pleasure whatsoever in the death of the wicked, Ezekiel tells us (Ezekiel 18:23 and 32) but He really enjoys showing mercy. He is not reluctantly merciful. He takes every opportunity to forgive where He can do it without being in conflict with other aspects of His nature.

📖 *Read: Micah 7:18.*

❓ **Question**: How does this principle relate to Luke 6:36?

## OUR GOD IS A MERCIFUL
## AND GRACIOUS GOD !

God forgives us not because He has to, but because He wants to. He gives us good things not out of obligation, but of His free will. If He treated us with strict justice, He would condemn us all. If He gave us, mankind, what we deserved, we would know the sharp end of His anger. Every act of kindness from a holy God towards sinful people is an expression of His grace. That means 'undeserved favour'.

God's love, grace and mercy are worked out towards us in that He, our Creator, Redeemer and King makes us (previously His enemies because of our sin and rebellion) into His own children. He in effect adopts us.

📖 *Read and meditate: 1 John 3:1.*

As we have become His children He treats us with long-suffering and patience. He is committed to us, will never abandon us; He puts up with all our faults and weaknesses and still loves us! Even His chastening is in love.

📖 *Read: Psalm 86:15, Lamentations 3:22-24, Ephesians 1:7-8, 2: 8-9, and 1 Peter 1:13.*

## OUR GOD IS A PATIENT GOD
## – HE IS LONG-SUFFERING

He cannot be anything else. It is His very nature. We have already seen that another key part of God's nature is that He can be totally relied upon. Faith is us relying on God. He is

71

utterly faithful to His truth. In Numbers 22 we read an intriguing account of a prophet hired to contradict God's word of promise given to the Israelites. He could not do it, and contrary to His own wishes reaffirmed God's faithfulness to what He had already said. In Numbers 23:19-20, this aspect of God's character is described, as in Isaiah 49:14-16. It is rare for a woman to abandon her own baby – though in extreme cases of desperation, going right against all her motherly instincts, she may do it – but God will never deny His nature by going back on His commitment to His children.

*OUR UTTERLY FAITHFUL GOD BRINGS US*
*REAL HOPE – FOR NOW AND THE FUTURE*

📖 *Read: Hebrews 6:13-20. In verses 17 and 18 God goes to extreme lengths to affirm His own faithfulness and steadfast unchangeable reliability.*

❓ **Question**: How would you explain this to your next-door neighbour?

## KNOWING AND BEING LIKE GOD

Obviously there are some ways in which we can never be like God. For example we can never have His omnipresence, omnipotence, or omniscience, but we can start to reflect His holiness, righteousness, goodness, love, mercy, grace, patience and faithfulness.

Although God is complex and mysterious, too big for us to grasp, we can know about Him and we can also know Him personally. We will discover that His character is true, as we begin to correctly interpret the experience of God in our lives.

## KEY POINTS ABOUT THE GOD WE WORSHIP

1. God asked the question, 'To whom will you liken me?' There is only one correct answer – 'No one'.

2. God cannot be categorised in human terms (e.g. tolerant, stern, broad-minded, easy-going, harsh). He is far, far bigger than that! He is far, far bigger than we can comprehend!

3. How do the following words describe what you have learned about God? Perfect, honest, fair, pure, loyal. What words would you add?

4. God is good and perfect. This is a truth, which has been made difficult for us by the debasing of the word 'good' in modern English. 'God is good' is the most common Biblical statement of God's perfection!

5. God is ever-present, everywhere and exists from eternity past to eternity future.

6. God is holy, righteous and just. Normally we do not use the word 'good' in this sense!

7. God is love.

❓ **Question**: Can you find other words to describe God's perfection meaningfully and accurately to a non-Christian friend?

# Week 5:
# THE TRUE NATURE
# OF MAN – GOD'S VIEW

## GROUP WORK SECTION

This week will consist of the following discussion on how each member 'got on' with their individual tasks. They are:

1. Prayer and fasting

2. The memory verse (1 Peter 5:7)

3. The individual Bible study

After this discussion your study leader will go through last week's individual study entitled 'A loving caring God?'. He will ask each to outline the answers they have given and the conclusions reached. This will involve general discussion as the review of last week's work proceeds.

The study leader will then outline the individual tasks for next week. They are:

– Individual Bible study that will help you to an understanding of man as God sees him. Again work through the study during the week and be ready to share your answers and conclusions next week.

– Individual prayer target. Try and spend at least 20-30 minutes each day in prayer. Develop a suitable structure for your prayer activity.

– Try once again to fast for one day before the next group meeting. Concentrate your prayer efforts on persons known to you, perhaps family or friends, who do not yet know Jesus as their Savour. Pray for their conversion.

– Memorise two verses of Scripture: Romans 8:27-28.

## INDIVIDUAL WORK SECTION

This section is for individual study. Your conclusions and answers will be discussed at the next group meeting, as will those of other group members.

## FROM GOD'S VIEW OF THE WORLD: WHO OR WHAT AM I?

### WHAT IS A HUMAN BEING?

Probably one popular song more than any other sums up the true nature of modern man. A song that encapsulates the 'spirit of the age', an age that does not apparently 'want' or 'need' God. An age that thinks that 'we have got it all sorted out'. The song *'I did it my way!'*, the most well-known version of it sung by Frank Sinatra, is a hymn for, or to the worship of, hedonism – that is (selfish) personal pleasure.

Just as we have tried to discover what God is like by finding out what He says about Himself, so we will learn about ourselves by understanding what HE says about us.

If we just look at ourselves and each other to try and discover what (and who) mankind really is, we are likely to be baffled and confused. So far in this study the terms man and mankind have been used to refer to humanity, the human race and to both women and men equally. Recent awareness of gender-specific terms or language has rendered the term 'man' problematic to many women in particular. This is and should be an important issue for all, male and female, as one of the key things that Jesus did through His teaching was to raise the status of women to that of 'the irrelevance of gender' before God in terms of worth!

The approach that has been followed in this study, is to seek a balanced view of what the Bible says. Using this approach, it is possible to identify in the Bible distinctive human characteristics.

Before doing this, it is worth noting that all world-views of the nature of man rely upon human narratives to understand the meaning of different cultures and provide a framework of reference. Both liberal humanism and Marxism – probably the two most powerful philosophies of the modern Westernised world – provide rather different world-views from that of traditional Bible-based Christianity. In the humanist world-view, everything is based on the rise of the autonomous and rational individual, with much talk of 'personal liberty' and 'personal choice'. In the case of Marxism, individuals are submerged in the 'needs of society', from which an identity is taken. Society in turn, for a Marxist thinker, is divided into classes, the development of which is usually dictated by the operation of 'historical dialectic'. To both of these non-Christian world-views, which in part have their roots in ancient Greek thinking, 'God is dead', that is they have no need or room for God. In contrast to this, biblical Christianity takes its reference point from God and the cross of Jesus Christ. The idea of 'the autonomy of man', or of 'the subjection of man to that of being a mere slave of society' are not biblical and therefore flawed, as they do not have a true foundation.

Both liberal humanism and until recently Marxism, strove but albeit in very different ways to build a new 'ideal society' based on amongst other things reliance on science, technology and innovation as instruments of reason and progress, together with education, democracy, rule of law, and medical science. It was believed that a capitalist or Marxist economic system could provide the wealth or materials for the new 'modern society'.

78

Modernity as it was called, was seen outside of religious belief and in particular Christianity, positively and optimistically as the only human hope. But something went wrong: total mechanised war (World Wars 1 and 2), the use of science to kill millions more effectively (e.g. fire bombs, chemical and nuclear weapons), pollution, world suffering and conflict, have caused disillusionment and a growing debate since the 1980's, in particular in the social sciences, termed 'post-modernism'. Is there evidence to suggest that a social transformation is taking place? Philosophers are now turning sceptically on their own 'modernist' doctrines (predictably so from a biblical perspective) as they are manifestly not working! They cannot – they are starting from the wrong position/point and therefore have a wrong world-view. The Bible makes this quite clear. Read 2 Timothy 4:3-4, is this a good description of post-modernism?

To the disillusioned post-modernist, the only certainty is that there are no absolutes – nothing is certain, and 'truth' is therefore dismantled. Today 'modern man', whether he realises it or not, takes his identity from: his lifestyle, what he consumes, the car he drives, the quality of house he lives in, clothes he wears and the sort of holiday he takes as well as the people, the group or the 'clan' he mixes with. Many within the post-modern movement embrace the nihilism (total rejection of all current beliefs in religion and morals) of Friedrich Nietzsche. That is, as old values crumble, new groups with a different (equally valid) world-view will emerge, but never be quite able to agree on the common good. So new 'alliances', loose confederations of 'tribal groups' emerge, under emotive and often very laudable banners of 'environmental protection' or similar. In the post-modern world, the battle cry has been 'my world-view is just as valid as yours'.

Perhaps because modern Bible-based Christianity has been so strongly (and wrongly) locked into middle-class, white, wealthy, educated male symbols in the Westernised world, it has made little significant contribution to the post-modern debate. However the fact remains, that 'truth', and in particular God's truth, is NOT a matter of our personal opinion. It is revealed truth that has been clearly given to us by God (the Holy Spirit) through the Prophets and the Apostles, that is the key. Although we will need to rethink HOW we PRESENT the gospel for each age, it is vital that we make sure that the truths, the absolutes behind the message never change! This is why as Christians we each need to have a good grasp of them, because they are just as relevant now (today and tomorrow) as they ever were!

As you now study the Bible to seek out God's view of the true nature of God and man, prayerfully draw your own conclusions about the relevance of what Scripture has to say for the world today – our world, the world we live in!

Humanity has so much potential for good – and so much potential for evil: what a contrast is presented to us! What about human achievements? Has there been positive progress?

## ℘ **Questions**

1. Give an example in each area of human life known to you, where there has been positive progress in:
   - medicine
   - food production
   - political progress – democracy?
   - service to others
   - music or art
   - quality of life
   - a fairer world system
   - science and technology.

2. What about human failures? Describe areas where mankind has been less successful:

- economics

- ecology

- modern warfare, weapons and peacekeeping

- politics

- moral education/citizenship

- elimination of cruelty and oppression

- tolerance: racial, religious, national and cultural.

3. All of these are big issues, but what of us as individuals? Do we have any areas of personal success?

- A good relationship with a spouse or family member.

- An act of kindness to someone in need without reward.

- A useful contribution to my neighbourhood?

4. Do we have areas of personal failure?

- An example of selfishness?

- An example of anger?

- An example of greed or selfish ambition?

- An example of envy or jealousy?

- An example of negativeness or dissatisfaction?

Note that we are often keen to draw the veil over issues of immorality, theft, or dishonesty!

## WHAT IS THE TRUE NATURE OF MAN?

When we look at humanity in general and ourselves in particular, we get the same picture – tremendous potential, but a fatal flaw, so that man's best efforts are tarnished and the overall picture is generally negative.

What is perhaps surprising is that it is exactly how the Bible describes us – and even tells us how human beings became like it. God made the world and all that is in it. The central pinnacle and purpose of the whole of God's creative activity was – humanity, man and woman!

📖 *Read: Genesis 1:26-31. Observe that people were made in the image of God (verse 26) and that the whole creation, including humanity, was considered by God to be very good (verse 31).*

*WHAT MODEL DID GOD USE WHEN CREATING HUMANITY? HE CREATED THEM MEN WOMEN IN HIS OWN IMAGE!*

But what does the 'image of God' mean? If you look in the mirror you see an *image* of yourself. It is not actually you – but it is very like you in some important ways. But it is also unlike you in some important ways – for example, it is only two-dimensional and is dependent on the reflection of light from a light source. That reflection will cease if either the source of the light is obstructed or if you walk away from the mirror. In addition it is not a true reflection, but is a mirror image, that is left and right are reversed!

However, this mirror illustration describes humanity, God's creation, well – very much like God in some ways but very different in others! The human beings He created were like Him, in that they had individual personalities, free will, the ability to think independently and critically, the ability to analyse and to communicate and the ability for self-expression and creativity. In other ways humanity is very different from God, not all-powerful, not all-knowing and not eternal. In one other way we are very different – humanity's very existence depends on God, but God is quite independent and self-sufficient.

We have seen that God is not bound by time and space. That is He is outside of time (immortal) and physical space (omnipresent). He is not confined by a human type body, but has, however, the option of entering time and space if He so chooses. That is if He wanted to, He could confine Himself to the limitations of a human body and time.

*Read: Genesis 2. God gives us some more details of the process of creation and the Creator's original role for humanity.*

**Questions**:

    1. Where did humanity come from?

    2. What is the basis of our physical being?

    3. Where did the non-physical part of us come from?

After you have developed your answers to the three questions above using Genesis 2, answer 'Yes', 'No' or 'Don't know', to each of the five questions below:

**Questions**: Man is a body/spirit unity. What was he made for?

- to give pleasure to God?
- to work?
- to understand His creation (scientific discovery)?
- to satisfy himself?
- to serve others (each other)?

A few interesting things to ponder after reading Genesis 2:

1. Adam was created fully grown – a mature adult, ready for work!

2. Eve was created from Adam for him and they are mutually dependent.

Matthew Henry, a famous Bible teacher, writing 300 years ago expressed this point concerning Eve in the language of his day but with great insight:

> *Not out of his head to top him; not out of his feet*
> *to be trampled on by him; but out of his side to be*
> *equal to him; under his arm to be protected by*
> *him; and near his heart to be loved.*

As God originally created humanity, they had everything they needed for a perfect existence: plentiful food, rich in variety (Gen. 1:29), satisfying work, a warm loving friendship and the presence of God. There were no predators or other dangers; there was no pollution; a pleasant stable climate. Above all there was no guilt, regrets or troubled conscience. They were without shame or guilt – a perfect existence!

?   **Question**: What can we learn from this story from Genesis about the relationship between man and woman as originally planned by God?

## SO WHAT WENT WRONG WITH MANKIND?

What we have looked at so far accounts for the positive features of human life – but what went wrong?

📖 *Read: Genesis 3.*

In Genesis 3:1-19 there were three clear stages in the destruction of this perfect existence.

1. *Deception (v.1-5).* Identify the stages by which Satan beguiled Eve and brought about their downfall.

❓ **Questions**:
   - Is what Satan quoted really what God said? (v.1)
   - What was the significant difference between the two accounts?
   - Were there any other differences?
   - What aspects of God's character are called into question in verses 4 and 5?

2. *Disobedience (v.6).* Note how the conversation changes from 'a friendly chat with Satan', to outright dissent against God. Eve chose to believe the cunning words of Satan rather than those of God. She allowed herself to flirt with or want what was forbidden. She took the lead in bringing another believer into sin. Adam failed to act responsibly: he did not challenge, or ask questions; he 'followed the crowd' (of one!) and took the line of least resistance and in so doing, joined in the dissent.

3. *They have their eyes opened (v.7-8).* Having disobeyed God and eaten of the tree of life suddenly they have become like God in an unintended way. They had obtained the knowledge of

both good and evil – as promised (2:17). But instead of becoming like God (3:5) they now experienced intense insecurity, shame, guilt, fear and self-consciousness. They were awkward, no longer pure and holy so they were no longer peaceful and happy! Death was promised (Genesis 2:17 and 3:19) and from this moment on, they were mortal, spiritually dead – i.e. alienated from God and as a result their bodies began to age and die.

*Read: Romans 5:12-19 and 1 Corinthians 15:21-23. Here you have a description of Jesus the 'second Adam' providing a way out of the problems caused by the first Adam.*

**Questions**: What might have happened if they had not disobeyed God – in terms of their spiritual life together and with God and to their own physical bodies?

## ADAM AND EVE'S DISSENSION AGAINST GOD HAS CONSEQUENCES FOR ALL OF US – EVEN TODAY

As a result of the dissent, God's creation was contaminated – so much so that all their offspring, and that includes us, have been born with the image of God spoilt, that is spiritually and genetically defective.

**Question**: In what way can we see this around us?

We can see it all around us: at a world level, we see the greed that has transformed fertile regions or rain forests into deserts or wasteland; violence against other humans that for very many is a way of life or favourite form of entertainment; the sex industry in all its forms, which to hold on to its customers (addicts?) and their insatiable appetites, needs ever greater depravity. At a personal level, we see it in children, even very young children, who do not have to be taught to act in selfish and disobedient ways but who need to be taught and encouraged to do right. See Romans 1:18 – 2:16. Sadly, because of the sins of our ancestors each of us is born with fatal defects – we are contaminated (see also Romans 3:23). Here is the beginning of the explanation of the paradox that is mankind: immense potential – but with a self-destruct button!

## HUMANITY HAS IMMENSE POTENTIAL
## BUT ALSO A FATAL FLAW

It would be reasonable to expect God to give up on us completely – but amazingly this is NOT the case. We can therefore understand the Psalm writer (Ps. 8:4). He is genuinely surprised that God bothers with us!

In the Old Testament, we find time and time again that Creator God longing for His creation, His people, reaching out His hands to them, encouraging them in various ways to find Himself. In the book of Hosea (1:2), the prophet Hosea is asked by God to marry a prostitute who is constantly unfaithful, as an example of the love God bears for His unfaithful people. The heart of Jesus can be clearly seen in Luke 13:34, where He is grieving over Jerusalem.

Whilst considering this subject we should not forget that God despite all of this still loves His creation. Below are a number of ways in which the negative (fallen) side of our nature is expressed.

87

1. *How we think.* Modern science seeks explanations of how the world or an aspect of it works without any recognition of or reference to God!

2. *Motives (our hidden agendas).* Various pieces of research have shown that what restrains most from doing things they know to be wrong, is the fear of being found out! For example, research suggests that a majority would be unfaithful to their spouses, if they really thought that they could do it without being found out! Similarly within the anonymity of a crowd, people tend to behave very differently from that in situations where they can be clearly identified. As a result one way of controlling a crowd is to make the individuals within it feel vulnerable, that is when there is a chance that they can be identified, and thus held to account for their actions! Matthew 6:1-4 outlines another radically different way! What are the implications of these verses on your thoughts, personal agenda and actions?

3. *Our common sense and well-being.* One well-known saying goes something like this:

> *If we are not politically (and idealistically) left*
> *when we are young, we have no heart. If we are*
> *not politically right (and a touch cynical) when we*
> *are older, we have no sense.*

Putting to one side questions about whether such a saying is correct or not, it does at least have a point! The young are idealistic, romantic, a touch naïve and gullible, and there is nothing wrong with that. But years later a number of broken relationships or a bitter divorce or two, people are hurt, bitter and often cynical about human nature ('Men!!! or equally 'Women!!!).

Our emotions can become just as confused, disordered and damaged, simply from living in this fallen, fallible world around us. This can lead to many of us having serious emotional, stress or psychological problems. Perhaps we have recurring dreams, flashbacks, nightmares, big regrets, areas we cannot talk about, anger against someone who was close to us – someone that we had trusted, an inability to 'get close' even to someone we love dearly. Such reactions can be our natural self-protection, not wanting the risk of becoming vulnerable and possibly hurt again!

? **Questions**: Your own emotional state – how would you assess it?

- Can I express affection to people I care about in a helpful way?
- Does my anger (sudden or irrational) ever damage others?
- Can I get alongside those who are sad or depressed?
- Have I been hurt by the emotions (or lack of them) of others?
- Have I been badly hurt by a failed relationship?

4. *Our inner conscience.* Our inner conscience should exactly mirror the law or desires of God.

? **Questions**:

- How often is it ignored or suppressed?
- Do I rationalise things that I want to do, but if I stopped and listened to my conscience, I would know are wrong?

📖 *Read: Proverbs 28:13-14; Jonah 1:5; Romans 9:1; 1 Timothy 1: 18-20; 3: 8-9; 4: 1-2; 1 Peter 3: 13-17. What do these passages teach us about our conscience?*

89

5. *The human body*. For all of us eventually our bodies will succumb to the ageing process, sickness and death. Despite this gloomy outlook how should we treat our bodies in the light of what God has to say?

*Read: 1 Corinthians 6:15; 1 Thessalonians 5:23; Philippians 3:21; Colossians 3:4; 1 Corinthians 15:49; 1 Corinthians 3:16; 6:19; 2 Corinthians 6:16; Ephesians 2:22 and 1 Peter 2:5.*

# Week 6:
# SIN – AN OUT-OF-DATE
# CONCEPT OR WHAT?

## GROUP WORK SECTION

This week will consist of the following discussion on how each member 'got on' with their individual tasks. They are:

1. Prayer and fasting

2. The memory verse (Romans 8:27-28)

3. The individual Bible study

After this discussion your study leader will go through last week's individual study entitled 'The true nature of man – God's view'. He will ask each to outline the answers they have given and the conclusions reached. This will involve general discussion as the review of last week's work proceeds.

The study leader will then outline the individual tasks for next week. They are:

– Individual Bible study that will help you to develop an understanding of the true nature of sin. Again work through the study during the week and be ready to share your answers and conclusions next week.

– Individual prayer target. Try and spend at least 20-30 minutes each day in prayer. Develop a suitable structure for your prayer activity.

– Try once again to fast for one day before the next group meeting. Concentrate your prayer efforts on persons known to you, perhaps family or friends, who do not yet know Jesus as their Saviour. Pray for their conversion.

– Memorise another verse of Scripture: Romans 3:23.

This section is for individual study. Your conclusions and answers will be discussed at the next group meeting, as will those of other group members.


## SO... WHAT THEN IS SIN?

The Bible uses a range of terms to describe sin, covering such concepts as: falling short of the goal, breaking a relationship and rebellion against God. The common idea that unites these concepts is the notion of 'falling short of what God intends' or 'a turning away from God to something or someone lesser'.

So what does the Bible have to say about sin? Firstly it makes it clear that all human beings are sinners. There is a flaw in human nature. We are fallen beings in a fallen world. The quite radical implication of the Christian view of both mankind and our world has fundamental consequences for our understanding of our ability to be moral leaders in society.

Below is a short summary of what the Bible has to say about sin, its effect on humanity and the consequences.

📖  *Readings:*

- *The consequences of sin.* Read: Genesis 3:1-19.

- *God cannot ignore sin.* Read: Exodus 32 and 34.

- *The role of our conscience.* Read: 2 Samuel 24:10-15.

- *We must confess all sin to God.* Read: Ezra 9: 5-15.

- *We must ask God for forgiveness.* Read: Psalm 51.

- *Sin has a beginning.* Read: Proverbs 1:10-19; Matthew 5: 27-28; James 1:15; 4:17.

- *Every one of us has sinned*. Read: Romans 3:23.

- *Sin results in death*. Read: Romans 6:23.

- *Jesus paid the price for our sin*. Read: Romans 8: 1-2; 1 John 1: 8-9.

There are two kinds of sin: 'the sin of Adam', the sin we inherit, the fatal flaw (like an inherited defective gene).

📖 *Read: Romans 5:12*

This means that man's natural state is that of alienation from God, in which the love of self takes the place of love of God. The other kind of sin is what some in the church call the sins of commission (doing what we should not do) and omission (not doing what we should do). In either case they are linked to the 'sin of Adam', since we fall short of what God intends, or turn from God's standard to a lower standard.

Many find the concept of 'the sin of Adam' a difficult one to accept. *'If God is a loving God,'* they say, *'how can He create people who He knows are doomed from birth?'* It seems that many are more ready to accept the results of their own actions, but feel somehow it is unfair, even unloving, that all are condemned from birth. If for discussion purposes we accept what the Bible says about mankind as being doomed from birth, as difficult as it is; then the key question is surely, *'If there is a loving God out there, and if He does love mankind His creation as He says He does, what has He done about it?'*

The Christian gospel by contrast centres on the key fact that, through the voluntary death and bodily resurrection of Jesus Christ (God's only Son), Christians are able to break free from this state of sin. The New Testament makes it clear however that salvation, although clearly begun in this life (new spiritual birth), will not be complete until Jesus' second coming, when our mortal bodies will be replaced (1 Corinth. 15: 50-53). Decisive progress can however be made in this life, when by faith and with the power of the Holy Spirit the believer begins to 'break the power of forgiven sin'. Christians are therefore those who are *being* saved.

📖 *Read: 2 Corinth. 2:15; Acts 2:47 and 1 Corinth. 1:18.*

For each of us, personal faith, through personal conversion, has five clear stages. They are:

1. *Confession* – admitting we are wrong unreservedly and asking God's forgiveness.

2. *Repentance* – a change of mind leading to a changed lifestyle. God will change your life if you are willing to change your mind, willing to turn from what is wrong and very deliberately walk away from the sin, vowing to resist with all we are.

3. *Believing* – asking God to come into our lives and committing our future to Him.

4. *Baptism in water* – a public confession of faith, no turning back.

5. *Being filled with the Holy Spirit* – the indwelling of God, empowerment, anointing for the future. The Spirit of God within that gives us the power to overcome the things we have renounced.

Each of these five steps can be undertaken quietly alone and in prayer. However once you have completed them you should tell another Christian as quickly as possible – ideally a church leader.

🅟 **Questions**:

1. Have you been through each of these stages fully?

2. Can you describe what happened at each stage?

3. How would you describe your conversion to a non-Christian friend?

This idea of being saved is a difficult and for some a contentious issue. It can be accurately summed up by the story of a young teenager, who asked her grandfather, 'Are you saved granddad?' to which he replied: 'I have *been* saved from the punishment for my sin! I am *being* saved from the power of sin on my life! One day I *will be* saved from the temptations caused by sin!' A good answer to a difficult question!

To put it simply, human beings are sinners. There is a flaw in human nature that can be seen in the world around us that has been created or altered by human beings. The bland assumption by Marxists and humanists, of the natural goodness of human nature so characteristic of much of modern Western liberal thought, demands the need for someone or something to blame (capitalists, multinationals, religion or a corrupt political system). Both Scripture and the evidence all around us challenge such conclusions, which have led to post-modernist 'thinking'. The evidence of the savagery and cruelty of the 20th century have challenged the myth of human perfectibility and inevitable progress.

Post-modernist commentators have analysed the evidence correctly from a biblical perspective. But in failing to understand the true nature of the traditional Christian gospel as outlined in Scripture, they have not realised that there is an answer: that there is hope and that there is an exciting way forward for mankind!

📖 *Read: Deut. 6:5 and Luke 10:25-37.*

Sin is first and foremost against God (see Psalm 51). We cannot hide it from Him; we are guilty and are personally responsible before God for our sinful attitudes and acts, which are the result of our flawed nature.

❓ **Questions**: List and describe the different ways in which sin is described in Psalm 51. How would you explain this list to a neighbour?

Earlier we said that many find the concept of 'the sin of Adam' a difficult one to accept. They argue: *'If God is a loving God,'* they say, *'How can He create people who He knows are doomed from birth?'* We have seen that the Bible says that although mankind is doomed from birth, there is a way out, that there is an answer to the question we posed earlier: *'If there is a loving God out there, and if He does love mankind His creation as He says He does, what has He done about it?'* Simply because of His love for humanity – His creation, God the creator sacrificed the most precious thing He had: His only Son, whom He loves more that we can comprehend. He did this to provide a way out of this problem – for us.

Contemplate on the immensity of God's love for us!

## THE PROBLEMS THAT SIN HAS CAUSED

All sin is offensive to God. Sin leads to guilt in us, but frequently has much wider consequences. The failure of one generation to measure up to God's standard will have repercussions on the next! The ruthless personal ambitions of politicians or multinational companies, or the personal short-termist greed of employers, will lead to cynicism and resentment in the population. Active rebellion by some will incite a violent retaliation by others. Short-termism, personal greed, ruthless personal ambition and impatience cause the environment to be polluted; dishonesty promotes mistrust; and the rejection of God's rules, His order and authority means that few people have any point of reference for living. The whole environment, as it is moulded by humanity often over many years, is therefore fatally flawed, damaged or as the Bible puts it 'contaminated by sin'.

📖 *Read: Exodus 20:5; Isaiah 24:5; Jeremiah 31:29-30; Romans 8:20, 22.*

❓ **Question**: Try to decide the biblical view on the following statements:

1. The world if left to itself will get better.

2. Animals are sinners too.

3. Children are in effect punished for their parents' sin.

4. Children can suffer from the consequences of their parents' sin.

❓ **Questions**: Are there any examples you can find in Scripture that illustrate the conclusions that you are coming to? How would you describe each of the above to a non-Christian friend?

## THE CHRISTIAN BELIEVER'S BATTLE WITH SIN

### Where does this battle take place?

It begins in the mind; the battle is subtle and often starts long before we realise.

98

📖 *Read: 2 Samuel Chapters 11 and 12. This is a sad but typical case study – as you will discover, the principles are just as relevant for today as they were then.*

## THE BATTLE WITH SIN – A CASE STUDY

*David was restless. He did not go off to war with Joab and Israel's army. He had 'done' that! He was bored; subconsciously he was looking for something new, different, exciting, and perhaps illicit? David probably knew that he should have gone with his troops, but it was his army, he was King and he could do what he wanted!*

*In this frame of mind, he had probably been more than a little careless about his 'prayer and praise' life and the time he spent reading the Scriptures each day. That is, he had neglected his relationship with God.*

*Walking restlessly on his roof garden, his eyes spotted Bathsheba. It is at the second and subsequent 'looks' that the sin begins. His eyes 'locked on to' Bathsheba; he wanted, and he desired what he should not have. The sin had started in the eye, gone to the mind, to the heart and then to actions that in turn lead to even worse sin, as he 'dug himself in' deeper and deeper. Pride and self-justification got involved as events then took over, events that resulted in the murder of Bathsheba's husband Uriah.*

*Later, after being confronted by Nathan, David confessed his guilt and God forgave him. David showed very real remorse and repentance. However, although God had forgiven the sin, David still had to live with the very real consequences of the sin he had committed.*

📖 *Read about David's remorse in Psalm 51. Read also about the consequences of the sin in 2 Samuel 12: 11; Psalm 3; 2 Samuel 13 and 15.*

❓ **Questions**:

1. What were the consequences of David's sin?

2. Whom did it affect?

It is interesting but also reassuring, that God brought good out of this sad situation.

📖 *Read: 2 Samuel 12: 24-25. Eventually David 'sorted himself out' before God, went to Rabbah and 'lead from the front', as he should have done in the first place! God gave him a wonderful victory! Read 2 Samuel 12: 26-31.*

## BUT DOES GOD THINK THAT MAN IS WORTH SAVING?

Is it all 'doom and gloom'? Do we have a fatally damaged world, heading for (self) destruction; populated by a humanity with a fatal flaw; living with the consequences of both their ancestors' and their own sins?

Scripture tells us *the loving God out there really does love mankind His creation as He says He does. He has solved the problem (which was not of His own doing) in a very wonderful act of pure love, but in a way that was very costly to Him personally.*

📖 *Read: Romans 5:17-19.*

We will look at the details of how this came about later – but for now let us just grasp the fact that when God comes into our lives, things are changed! We are transformed as the Holy Spirit begins to change us – but more of that later. However, each of the verses below contains at least one blessing/benefit of new life in Jesus Christ. See if you can match the verse with the blessing/benefit!

## THE BLESSING/BENEFITS

We are:

- made alive by union with Christ (born again);

- justified (forgiven, declared righteous);

- no longer subject to death (will be given a new body when Jesus returns to earth);

- reconciled to God (Jesus being the interface between us and God);

- made God's children by adoption (become part of the invisible church);

- given new hearts (our value systems and desires will change);

- given new natures (gradually or suddenly we will be able to control things like a bad temper);

- given a new Spirit (have the Spirit of God in us);

- becoming new creatures (become noticeably different people);

- given eternal life (hope of a place forever in Heaven with Jesus).

📖 *Readings: A selection of verses is:*
- Ezek 36:26
- Ezek 36:27
- John 3:36
- Romans 5:8-9
- Romans 6:23
- Romans 8:15-17
- 2 Corinthians 5:7
- Ephesians 2:5
- Ephesians 2:13

God does not deal with 'humanity' as a group or by nations – but with individuals. Individually, everything that was spoilt at or by the Fall (Adam and Eve's falling into sin) can be restored to us in Jesus Christ. However we still live in a fallen world! That is why life for the Christian involves conflict, trials, hard work, and sometimes great suffering (John 16:33). Like David we have for now to live with and face up to the consequences of our sin.

❓ **Questions**:

1. What consequences of my own sin do I now have to live with and face up to?

2. How should I do it as a Christian?

Once God through Jesus has transformed us, He will not allow us to destroy ourselves again, provided that we ask Him for help to overcome our personal sin when we are tempted. The way God restores us we will look at in another session.

❓ **Questions**: Some final concluding questions on this section:

1. What does the Bible say about man in Genesis 1:26-31; 2:7-15?

2. What does 'in our image, after our likeness' mean?

3. What did God mean by calling man 'good'?

4. What was God's purpose in creating man? Acts 17:26,27; Mark 12:28-34.

5. What does it mean in very practical terms 'to love God with all my heart, all my understanding and all my strength'?

6. What does it mean in very practical terms 'to love my neighbour as myself'?

7. In what ways does Adam's sin committed so long ago affect us? Romans 5:12-14; Job 14:1,4; Psalm 51:5; John 3:16.

8. What is the Bible's verdict on man's nature? Romans 1:18-21; 3:10-18; 1 John 1:8

9. How does the above compare with the current popular world-view of humanity?

A meditation:

> *Given the true nature of humanity, what sort of love is it that causes the creator to prepare such a self-sacrificial way back to Himself, for each individual human being no matter what he or she has done? ('He knows the worst about us, but loves us just the same.')*

# Week 7:
# JESUS A MAN, GOD, OR BOTH?

## GROUP WORK SECTION

This week will consist of a brief discussion on how each member 'got on' with their individual tasks:

1. Prayer and fasting

2. Memory verse (Romans 3:23).

3. Individual study

After the brief discussion, your study leader will then talk through last week's individual study entitled 'Sin – an out-of-date concept or what?' He will ask each to outline the answers they have given and the conclusions reached. This will involve general discussion as the review proceeds.

The study leader will then outline the individual tasks for next week. They are:

1. Individual Bible study that will help you to develop further your understanding of who Jesus was, the events surrounding His life and the relevance of them in the new millennium. Again you should work through the study and be ready to share your answers and conclusions next week.

2. Individual prayer target. Try and spend at least 30 minutes each day in prayer. Remember to develop a suitable structure for your prayer time.

3. Once again, try to fast for one day before the next group meeting. Focus your efforts around an issue such as praying for the church, its leaders and/or members.

4. Memorise another verse of Scripture – Galatians 2:20.

## INDIVIDUAL WORK SECTION

This section is for individual study. Your conclusions and answers will be discussed at the next group meeting, as will those of other group members.

## THE HISTORICAL JESUS CHRIST – WHO WAS/IS HE?

We have already discussed Jesus Christ when looking at His relationship to the Father and also as our link or gateway to God. We will now look in more detail at His origins, His purpose, His life, His death and what happened after He died.

### THE REAL JESUS – WHAT WAS OR IS HE LIKE?

This is a key question, as in effect the whole of Christianity hangs on the answer. From the time 2,000 years ago when Jesus asked the question, 'Who do people say that I am?' to the present day, there have been many answers. So which one is true?

In Matthew 16:14,16 in answer to Jesus' question, the disciples gave a summary of the various then current speculations: 'Some say John the Baptist [presumed risen from the dead]; some say Elijah, some Jeremiah and some say one of the prophets.' Jesus then asked who they (the disciples) personally believed Him to be. Simon Peter one of Jesus' closest followers answered, 'You are the Christ [Greek word for Hebrew 'Messiah'], the Son of the Living God.' Jesus then told Peter that he had not discovered this truth by human deduction or persuasion, but that His Heavenly Father (God) had revealed it to him personally.

Why did some think He was Elijah (who had died 800 years earlier)?

Why did some think He was Jeremiah (who had died 500 years earlier)?

Today there are many ideas about Jesus and behind them often lie 'hidden agendas' and ignorance. However none of them are supported by Scripture as being either an accurate or a complete picture.

Some modern ideas are:

1. He was a great teacher of ethics.

2. He was a deluded fanatic.

3. He was a deliberate impostor.

4. He was a good man, turned into a God by His followers.

5. He came from outer space – an alien.

6. He was a mythical invention.

**Question**: Who do you think Jesus is or was? What is your conviction based on?

    1. A balanced examination of the facts available?

    2. The clear conviction of others persuaded me?

    3. God showed it to me?

(More than one of these factors may be involved.)

## SO WHO THEN IS JESUS?

Jesus was regularly challenged as to who He was. From His own defence in these discussions, we discover His awareness of His own unique person.

In John 8:30-59 Jesus is challenged by the natural descendants of Abraham, to whom He made the (and to them blasphemous) reply, *'Before Abraham was, I AM'*, or in modern English, *'The truth is, I existed before Abraham was even born.'* This is more than just affirming that He existed prior to Abraham (Abraham had died approximately 2,000 years earlier).

📖 *Read: Exodus chapter 3; John 8:58; John 10:22-31; John 14:5-14.*

❓ **Questions**:

1. What exactly was Jesus claiming in John 8:58?

2. The charge of blasphemy (indicated by the attempt by the crowd to carry out the sentence in John 8:59) is made again as recorded in John 10:22-31. The implications of v.30 were certainly clear to His listeners! What do you think Jesus meant in v.30? When talking to His own followers, in order to dispel their doubts and fears, He was quite explicit.

3. What are the implications of Jesus' reply in verses 6 and 7 of John 14: 5-14 to Thomas in respect of other religions then and today?

4. What does His reply to Philip in verses 9-14 indicate about His relationship with the Father?

Many people often have inflated ideas of their own importance! It is therefore important to hear what other people said about Jesus. Below are listed a few from His contemporaries. Read what they said and answer the questions.

❓ **Questions**:

1. *John the Baptist* (Read John 1:29-34). What does this passage teach about: the purpose of Jesus (v.29); the

pre-existence of Jesus (v.30); the nature of His being (v.34)

2. *Thomas the Doubter* (Read John 20:24-29). Do you think Thomas gave the right answer in v 28? If you said 'No', why do you think Jesus did not put him right?

3. *Pontius Pilate*, the Roman Governor (Read John 19:1-22). What did Pilate affirm as to Jesus' guilt (v.4,6), (Luke 23:4) and what were the implications behind Pilate's fear? (John 19:8). What do you think he meant by His preoccupation with Jesus' Kingship (v.11-12,14,19-22)? And whom did Pilate fear most?

4. What did *Pilate's wife* think of Jesus? (Matt. 27:19).

5. What did the battle-hardened *Roman officer* think of Jesus? (Luke 23:47).

6. Who did Jesus' bitterest enemies, *the demons*, think He was? (Read Matthew 8:28-29; Mark 1:23-26; 3:11 and Luke 4:41.) Note that three times they use the expression 'The Son of God'. What two other titles are used by them?

We have a choice. Anyone who makes claims to be uniquely the Son of God and who then receives worship as God must either be a madman, an impostor or a deceiver! Unless that is these astonishing claims are actually true. To say therefore that Jesus was simply a good man really does not fit the evidence.

Jesus is the Christ, the promised Messiah, God's Son.

And Jesus is Christianity. It is therefore important to know and understand as much as is revealed in the Bible about Him. This is so that as we personally get to know Him better, we can give Him the honour and respect which is due. Jesus is God!

## IF JESUS IS THEREFORE GOD – HOW THEN WAS HE A MAN AS WELL?

The clear implication of our study so far is that Jesus Christ, who was obviously regarded by those close to Him as a man, is also *the Son of God*. He was and is also God! That is He was and is *fully* God and *fully* man!

This means that the Almighty, Eternal, Unchanging, Holy, Perfect, Self-existent God, mysteriously and voluntarily allowed Himself to become limited by the dimensions of space and time and *chose* to be born at a particular point in history. He therefore took on a mortal body, affected by time, cold, hunger, pain and sin.

In a single phrase: GOD BECAME MAN AS WELL!

The hymn writer Charles Wesley put it very well when he wrote: *'Our God contracted to a span, incomprehensibly made man!'*

This God-man is called JESUS CHRIST

We should now stop for a minute and think about what we have just discussed. What we are now considering is more amazing than the creation of the Universe itself. The creator God voluntarily becomes part of His creation. Why did God do it? Why did the being that created the Universe limit Himself to time and space and in the Middle East, and on earth, one tiny part (speck?) of His immense creation?

## JESUS ALWAYS GOD – BUT NOT ALWAYS MAN!

We must remember that the man called the Lord Jesus was always God, but not always man. This is described in a number of ways in the Bible.

📖 *Read John 1:1-5. In this, for some, a difficult passage, we learn that the 'Word' being with God, being God, being the Creator, being the source of life and the source of light is a revelation to us. Who was this 'Word'?*

📖 *Read Colossians 1:15-21. The context makes it clear that the one who is the (visible) image of the invisible God is Jesus Christ.*

We not only have a reminder of His creative power but that it was all made for Him and that He holds it together. In fact Jesus has 'the pre-eminence in all things'.

📖 *Read: John 17:1-5. In v.5 we have recognition of the eternal glory and bliss that He had previously enjoyed and shared with the Father before becoming a human being.*

A strong desire to return to that state is also expressed. He quite deliberately left it all behind when He, God, became man.

## GOD TOOK ON HUMAN NATURE
### – HE BECAME FULLY MAN

📖 *Read: John 1:14. This takes us back to the idea of the eternal 'Word' or creative person/part of God, who was with God and who was God. Now we read that He became flesh, and lived among us as He took upon Himself mortal human nature.*

We learn from these verses of His 'pre-existence', that is before time began He already existed, of His direct involvement in creation, and of His 'becoming a human being'. Consider the infinite and eternal God restricting Himself to be expressed in a human life! He became a man, but never ceased to be God, though He chose not to exercise the power and rights of the Godhead for a season.

For Him to be *fully* man He had to be born. But how could the eternal God be born? And if born, would He not then inherit the defects of human nature?

📖 *Read: Matthew 1:18-25. This is the account from Joseph's point of view – the explanation for His fiancée's pregnancy – in spite of her still being a virgin.*

📖 *Read: Luke 1:26-38. This describes Mary's experience – and in v.35 we have the nearest thing to an explanation of what happened. Jesus was born in a unique way. The Holy Spirit conceived Jesus in the womb of Mary, replacing the human father, so that she gave birth as a virgin.*

The two natures, Divine and Human are distinct, not confused, but exist in tension. He is only one person but still perfect God and perfect Man! While existing as man on Earth He still retained the attributes, the qualities and characteristics of God, though His Godhead could be said to be often 'veiled' by His human nature.

## THE ATTRIBUTES OF JESUS

Such attributes or qualities as His eternal pre-existence have already been touched on.

℘   **Question**: What attribute or quality of the Godhead is referred to in each of the following verses? Remember they are: glory, holiness, omniscience, omnipresence, omnipotence, immutability etc. The verses are:

- John 2:24-25

- John 21:17

- Matthew 18:19-20

- Matthew 19:26

- Matthew 28:18-20

- Hebrews 10:10-18

- Hebrews 13:8

- Philippians 3:21

- Colossians 2:9

℘   **Question**: The full deity of the man, Jesus Christ, is often said to be clearly affirmed in Scripture. Do you think the following verses support this view?

- Romans 9:5

- Ephesians 3:19

- Philippians 2:5-11

- Titus 2:2-14

- 1 John 5:20

℘   **Question**: Jesus is recorded as being active before His human birth – Colossians 1:15-23 is one of many such references – but includes items only implied elsewhere in Scripture. What significant items of Jesus' work (e.g. creation) are mentioned in this passage?

Another aspect of Jesus' work in His role as God, is the forgiveness of sin (not just forgiving on a one-to-one for a personal matter). Read Mark 2:1-10. This describes an incident where Jesus' authority to forgive sin was challenged. How did Jesus define/describe His authority? Another Divine work ascribed to Jesus is 'The Final Judgement'.

📖 *Read: 2 Timothy 4:1 and compare with Matthew 7:21-23.*

❔ **Question**: Who makes the final decision about our eternal destiny?

Jesus alone fully expresses the nature of God in a way comprehensible to humans, not just in word only but as 'the Word made flesh'. That is to say not just a description of God, but a real living manifestation of God the Father. In writing to the Hebrews, Paul expresses so clearly the difference between the revelation of God that had come through the prophetic word and the infinitely more glorious revelation through the Son – Jesus.

This description can be found in Hebrews 1:1-3.

❔ **Questions**:

1. In what way was the previous revelation in the Old Testament not yet complete?

2. In what way is the revelation of His Son in the New Testament, building on that in the Old Testament, now complete?

*THE MAN JESUS CHRIST IS FULLY GOD*

Notwithstanding many spurious claims that Jesus is/was not God, the clarity and emphasis of Scripture on the divinity of Jesus Christ has led some to doubt or question the nature of His manhood. How could He be really human? Was His humanity just an illusion? Was it the Divine Spirit in a human body? All of these questions are valid – so we need to seek answers from the Bible.

1. *His conception and birth.* His conception was by modern medical understanding (to date anyway) 'unusual' since it would require a missing Y-chromosome to be supplied for a conception to take place. Although His mother was a virgin, His birth was normal and He was a very 'ordinary' baby. Read about this in Luke 2:6-7.

2. *His early years.* Read Luke 2:51-52. He grew up and developed as such a normal person, that for the major part of His public ministry, His own family did not recognise His uniqueness and the people of His home town referred to Him as the 'carpenter's son'. (See Mark 6: 1-6.)

3. *His sufferings.* Satan cunningly and strongly tempted him. Read about this in Matthew 4:1-11. He was often tired. Read about this in Mark 4:38. He knew real hunger. Read about this in Matthew 21:18. He knew serious thirst. Read about this in John 4:6-7. He knew great pain. Read about this in Luke 22:44. He knew deep sadness too. Read about this in John 11:35.

**Questions**:

1. What kind of person are we reading about here, a man or some kind of superhuman?

2. In the passages above do you detect a very human side to Jesus?

📖 *Read: John 4:34; Luke 22:42. A very important point to note is the complete obedience that Jesus showed to the will of His true father (God)!*

We will now look at just how vital it was that Jesus should be both divine and human in the full sense, in order to accomplish completely the work God sent Him to do.

Jesus Christ is only one person, but His deity and humanity combine to form a *unity*, NOT a *dual personality*. The clear underlying teaching of the New Testament points to this fact.

The two natures of Jesus, divine and human, are not confused or mixed, but remain quite distinct. Sometimes one appears to predominate, sometimes the other.

❓ **Question**: Which of the two predominant natures is most evident in the following examples?
- Mark 11:15-17
- Mark 13:32
- Luke 10:38-42
- John 18:6

Here again we are considering things that are quite beyond the capacity of our human minds to understand. We can do little more than receive the revelation as given to us – God is God and He did create the Universe! However a real danger arises when out of a desire to comprehend the infinite, either we speculate, going beyond what Scripture reveals, or in our impatience to know or our over-confidence about our understanding, we only see part of the truth and mistake it for the whole. This is an important point and should be noted.

At the beginning of this section, in several different ways, we asked the question: *Is Jesus a man, God, or is He both?*

117

In this section based on the evidence that can be found in Scripture, it has been shown that:

*JESUS CHRIST IS BOTH FULLY GOD
AND FULLY MAN!*

## SOME CONCLUSIONS ABOUT WHO JESUS IS

Here are some Old Testament prophecies concerning the coming of Jesus the Messiah.

*Concerning the Kingship of Jesus:*

– Psalms 2:6-8; 68:18; 118:22

– Isaiah 9:6-7; 32:1-2; 42:1-4

– Jeremiah 23:5

– Daniel 2: 44; 7:13-14

– Micah 5:2

– Zechariah 6:12-13; 9: 9-10

– Malachi 3:1.

*Concerning the suffering of Jesus:*

– Psalms 22:18; 69:21

– Isaiah 50:6; 52:14; 53:1-10

– Daniel 9:26

– Zechariah 11:2; 12:10; 13:7.

? **Question**: How do such clear prophesises of Jesus' first coming add to our understanding of who He is?

118

There are very many prophecies of Jesus' first coming listed in the Old Testament. Below are listed just a few of them, but in addition are listed New Testament references that show how they were fulfilled.

- 'Jesus will descend from the tribe of Judah'. See: Genesis 49:10 and Luke 3:33 and Matt 1:2-3.

- 'The heir to the throne of David'. See: Isaiah 9:7; 11:1-5; 2 Samuel 7:13 and Matthew 1:1-6.

- 'Jesus' birth place'. See: Micah 5:2 and Matthew 2:1; Luke 2:4-7.

- 'Born of a virgin'. See: Isaiah 7:14 and Matt 1:18; Luke 1:26-35.

- 'Triumphal entry'. See: Zechariah 9:9; Isaiah 62:11 and John 12:12-14; Matt 21:1-11.

- 'Betrayed by a friend'. See: Psalm 41:9 and Mark 14:10; Matt 26:14-16; Mark 14:43-45.

- 'Sold for thirty pieces of silver'. See: Zechariah 11:12-13 and Matthew 26:15; 27:3-10.

- 'Money to be returned for a potter's field'. See: Zechariah 11:13 and Matt 27:3-10.

- 'Crucified with sinners'. See: Isaiah 53:12;Matthew 27:38; Mark 15:27-28; Luke 23:33.

- 'His hands and feet pierced'. See: Psalm 22:1; Zechariah 12:10 and John 19:37; 20:25-27.

- Given gall and vinegar'. See: Psalm 69:21; Matthew 27:34,48; John 19:29.

- 'Prays for His enemies'. See: Psalm 109:4; Isaiah 53:12 and Luke 23:34.

- 'His side to be pierced'. See: Zechariah 12:10 and John 19:34.

- 'Soldiers cast lots for His clothes'. See: Psalm 22:18; Mark 15:24; John 19:24.

- 'No broken bones'. See: Exodus 12:46; Psalm 34:20; John 19:33.

- 'Buried with the rich'. See: Isaiah 53:9; Matthew 27:57-60.

- 'His bodily resurrection'. See: Psalm 16:10; Matthew 16:21; Matthew 28:9; Luke 24:36-48.

- 'His ascension back to the father'. See: Psalm 68:18; Luke 24:50-51; Acts 1:9.

**Question**: So then to sum up – in what ways does the Bible picture of Jesus differ from the current popular everyday view of Jesus?

Hint: try and answer this question in two ways:

1. As if you were explaining to an adult non-believer neighbour.

2. As if you were explaining it to a young person between 9 and 12 years of age.

*Some further readings: Isaiah 9:1-7; John 1:1-14; Philippians 2:5-11; Hebrews 1:1-14.*

# **Week 8**:
# **JESUS ROSE BODILY**
# **FROM THE DEAD**
# **– SO WHAT DOES IT MEAN?**

## GROUP WORK SECTION

This week will consist of a brief discussion on how each member 'got on' with their individual tasks:

1. Prayer and fasting

2. Memory verse (Galatians 2:20).

3. Individual study

Next, your study leader will go through last week's individual study entitled 'Jesus – a man, God, or both?' Each in turn will be asked to outline the answers they have given and the conclusions reached. This will involve some general discussion as the review proceeds.

The study leader will then outline the individual tasks for next week. They are:

1. The next individual Bible study, that will help you develop further your understanding of the death of Jesus and His resurrection. Again, work through the next study and be ready to share your answers and conclusions next week.

2. Individual prayer target. Try and spend a minimum of 30 minutes each day in prayer. Remember to prepare a prayer list to help you use your prayer time effectively.

3. Again, try to fast for one day before the next group meeting. Focus your efforts around an issue such as praying for physical healing or an issue that is currently being faced by people in your church fellowship who you know.

4. Memorise another verse of Scripture (1 Peter 3:18).

## INDIVIDUAL WORK SECTION

This section is for individual study. Your conclusions and answers will be discussed at the next group meeting, as will those of other group members.

## WHY DID JESUS DIE – WAS IT PLANNED, A MISTAKE OR WHAT?

If Jesus is all that we have established in previous weeks that He is – why then did He have to die? Did He (God) really die? Were there hidden defects or weaknesses in His life – or did it just all go wrong? Does His death on the cross simply teach us how to fail graciously when beaten by our enemies or by events outside of our control?

### JESUS – HOW DID HE LIVE?

📖 *Read: Philippians 2:5-11. Jesus' life on earth consisted of a deliberate and voluntary humbling of Himself.*

❓ **Question**: Can you identify the key stages of His self-humbling?

1. He started as an equal, at one with God.

2. He put to one side all of the privileges of the Godhead.

3. He became a man with the limitations, suffering and hardships that that produced.

4. He accepted the fate of a criminal and allowed himself to be badly treated by the very creation he had brought into being.

Yet throughout His life Jesus expressed all of the perfection of the character of God, His Father. This point should be noted. It is Jesus' personal humility whilst under the call and service of God his father, that is very challenging. It is something for all Christians to remember, both new or of many years standing, whether a church worker or a successful and famous church leader.

**Question**: Which of the following aspects of God's character are most clearly shown in the following passages? For example, His love, grace, wisdom, righteousness and power:

- Matthew 22:15-22
- Luke 8:22-24
- Luke 8:40-56
- Matthew 21:12-13
- John 8: 3-11.

Jesus was the first and only man ever to fulfil the law of God. He succeeded where Adam and the rest of us failed. God's law is absolute; it expresses unchangeable qualities in God Himself, but its standards are too high for us to attain. The law cannot be modified; we cannot keep it and so are condemned by it. But the man Christ Jesus kept it!

*Read: Matthew 5:17-18. Christ fulfilled all God's righteous requirements and as a result, at last one human being has pleased God!*

Jesus was tempted to take a short cut to achieving His objectives of introducing the Kingdom of God.

  *Read: Matthew 4:1-11. Jesus fully resisted these temptations. He was tempted in every possible way but without once succumbing to sin.*

  *Read: Hebrews 4:14-16. Jesus was tempted to give up just before His death but overcame the temptation.*

  *Read: Luke 22:39-46. This vital stage was necessary so that He could be the complete Saviour for all who put their trust in Him.*

Jesus' victory over temptation simply means that a human being, a part of God's creation, has now utterly defeated Satan.

*Jesus fulfilled God's law in His life* – through what he achieved in His life, Jesus cancelled out the human defeat in the Garden of Eden. Jesus withstood temptation and reversed the consequences of that defeat in Eden by living a life without sin.

So therefore if anyone deserved the right to live it was Jesus.

However he died.

And in a humiliating and agonising way.


## SO THEN JESUS DIED – BUT WHY?

  *Read: Hebrews 10:1-10 and Romans 5:19. Jesus Christ offered Himself as a living sacrifice to God, a substitute for us.*

Before we look in more detail at what that actually means we need to look at the historical accounts of His death.

125

📖 *Read: John 19:28-42.*

❓ **Question**: List *three* clear statements from this passage which affirm His physical death – Jesus really did die. (See in particular 19:30, 33 and 40.)

His death was not only a physical death in the sense we understand. As He died He experienced the pain, the very torment of hell itself – that is being cut off from His Father, whose love and fellowship He had known continuously from eternity past. Read Mark 15:33-34; John 17:5. At this point he experienced suffering more severe than the physical pain, the naked humiliation of a criminal's death and the mockery of the crowds. In this experience of separation from God, He knew the full pain of hell. So what was accomplished by His sacrificial death on the cross?

In His life He fulfilled completely the law by keeping fully the commandments of His Father God. In His death He fulfilled the law of sacrifices – a perfect specimen offered in place of the guilty party. That is, his death paid the penalty for breaking the laws of the creator of the Universe, for all mankind, but also very much on an individual basis for each of us personally! If you jump off a 100m cliff onto the rocks below, within five seconds or so you will face rather abruptly the consequences of your action! As humans we sin in two ways: the sin caused by our inherited defective human nature (as discussed earlier) and called by Biblical scholars 'the sin of Adam'; and the actions that we take as a result of our own free will – 'personal sin'. In just the same way as the cliff jumper will have no choice but to face the sudden brutal and final consequences of his action, so too do we for our sin – a very sobering thought!

However there is good news – we can allow Jesus to include us in his list of those who he calls his own.

📖 *Read: John 3:16; 1 Corinthians 15:19; Titus 1:1-2; Romans 8:1-2. For those Jesus calls his own – he has paid the penalty and in full!*

## JESUS FULFILLED THE LAW OF GOD
## IN HIS DEATH

He was our substitute in life (doing what we could not do) and in death (being punished for what we have done).

📖 *Read: Isaiah 53:3-6. It is often forgotten that Calvary looks both backwards and forwards in respect of time. Don't forget that God is outside of time.*

Grace through Faith in fact saved Israel. God's grace could be given to them because from God's perspective the Lamb was slain before the foundation of the world.

📖 *Read: Revelation 13:8. It was not in fact the blood of bulls and of goats that saved them, for they alone could never take away sins.*

📖 *Read: Hebrews 10:1-10. As far as God was concerned, however, it was by the death of Christ that they were saved.*

As far as they were concerned, however, it was through faith (Abraham – Genesis 15:6) and obedience (to the ceremonial law, and the moral law); just as today the Atonement primarily speaks to God. It says punishment has been meted out. Justice has been done. God is reconciled to us.

127

📖 *Read: Romans 5:10; Colossians 1:20-21 and Ephesians 2:16. So too we are persuaded to be reconciled to God.*

📖 *Read: 2 Corinthians 5:18-20. Under the Old Covenant, the animal sacrifices in effect pointed forward in time and in a symbolic way to their fulfilment in Christ's sacrifice.*

When at Communion we break bread and drink the wine, we point back in time to that same sacrifice.

Therefore the penalty of sin has now been paid forever. It is finished and will never need to be paid again. There is no way in which we can, or need, to work our way to God through 'good works', purgatory, penance or anything else that is often fear driven. The clear and consistent message in the Bible is quite clear on this.

📖 *Read: John 19:30. If there had been any other way of redeeming a fallen race, then God would have found it! We can be sure that we will never find another way!*

📖 *Read: Hebrews 10:11-14.*

❓ **Questions**:

1. Why did the Old Testament sacrifices have to be repeated?

2. Why did Jesus' sacrifice not have to be repeated?

📖 *Read: Leviticus 16. What is being taught to the Israelites sheds light on the doctrine of sacrifice and helps us to understand the purpose of the death of Christ.*

⁊ **Questions**:

1. Why did Aaron have to make an offering for himself?

2. Why were two goats used?

So in very practical terms, what does that mean to us? Before we can fully appreciate what it means to us, we must understand what it meant to God the Father. God the Father sent Jesus on His great mission. It was in total obedience to GOD His Father that Jesus came.

God's law had been broken consistently by *every* member of the human race. Whatever else we may or may not have done none of us have loved God with all our heart, mind, soul and strength (as He requires of us) and so have broken at least one of His laws.

Can a loving and merciful God just overlook all our faults and forgive us? No – not without denying part of His own character (His righteousness and justice). Again the problem is our limited, finite human mind. We in our arrogance make God too small. We turn Him into a God we are happy/comfortable with. We don't, 'abandoning all', seek to know 'the one true God' as He really is. Like a small child we cover our eyes/mind and try to ignore what we don't like, or find uncomfortable – or worse, when the known facts about God do not fit into our personal 'world-view'. What arrogance we mankind have when facing a God so big, that the small part of his Universe that we know about is still so immense, that it would take 12 billion years for light to travel from one end to the other!

Also, for God to overlook our faults, would suggest that sin is not terribly serious and that forgiveness is cheap! How much more 'mind blowing' is that act of mercy which in showing how serious sin is and satisfying the demands of justice, God

Himself suffers on our behalf in the person of Jesus His Son? Read: Romans 8:32.

The Old Testament account of Abraham being willing to offer Isaac his own son in sacrifice helps us to understand a little of how God the Father must have viewed the sufferings of His own Son.

📖 *Read: Genesis 22:1-14. Notice especially how God would not allow Abraham to suffer the agony of sacrificing His son – but God went beyond what would be required of anyone else, and freely gave up His own Son for us!*

📖 *Readings: Read the verses of Scripture below, which describe some of the things that were achieved by the life and death of Jesus Christ, the Son of God.*

- Romans 3:21-26
- Romans 5:8
- Romans 5:18
- 2 Corinthians 5:19-20
- Hebrews 9:28
- Hebrews 10:12
- 1 Peter 1:18-19
- 1 Peter 3:18
- 1 John 4:10

Some useful hints:

- God and sinners reconciled.
- The love of God displayed to sinners.
- God's justice fully satisfied.
- The full redemption of the debt of sin.

- Christ as our substitute.
- Our sin borne by Jesus on the cross.
- The finality and the completeness of His sacrifice

As a very practical result of what Jesus did on the cross:

1. We can in prayer and worship go directly into the presence of God.

2. We have full forgiveness.

3. We have unconditional acceptance by God.

4. We have been adopted into His family (as children and heirs).

5. He has a special plan and purpose for each of our lives – something that only each of us with our unique skills and experiences can do.

6. We have the promise of everlasting life.

Each of the scriptures below relates to one of these benefits:

- 1 John 1:9
- Galatians 3:26
- John 3:16
- Romans 6:6-14
- Isaiah 53:3
- Hebrews 12:18-24

*BUT THE DEATH OF JESUS WAS NOT THE END: JESUS ROSE BODILY FROM THE GRAVE – THREE DAYS LATER!*

There are five separate biblical accounts of the bodily resurrection of Jesus on the Sabbath day, each originating from different eyewitness sources in ones and twos.

📖 Read: Matt 28:8-10; Mark 16:9; Luke 24:13-32 and 34; John 20:10-17.

There are seven further biblical accounts of His post-resurrection appearance before His ascension:

- The following Sunday in the Upper Room to all: John 20:19.
- At Galilee lakeside, as reminded by the angel at the tomb, with seven disciples: John 21
- On a mountain in Galilee to the 11 disciples: Matthew 28:16-20.
- On other occasions: Acts 1.
- To 500 brethren in one gathering: 1 Corinthians 15:6.
- To James, the half-brother of Jesus: 1 Corinthians 15:7.
- At the Ascension from the Mount of Olives: Acts 1:6-11.

The fact that He rose from the dead is beyond reasonable dispute. Historically there is probably more evidence to support this event, than there is to support many other important historical events that are rarely challenged! Most of those who challenge the resurrection have, if they are honest, their own (hidden) agenda for doing so. Personal lifestyle perhaps, or simply because they resent anyone, even the Creator of the Universe, telling them how to live *their* life!

As a point of interest – just how much is this widely held Western concept of 'personal freedom' in modern society real, or an illusion (delusion)? It could be the subject of a major and fascinating debate – but one for another time!

132

Those wanting 'to do their own thing', the post-modernists, in effect conduct a personal rebellion against God; they want to echo the words quoted earlier of Frank Sinatra, 'I did it my way'! Sadly, the Bible makes it all too clear, that such a decision or choice has a price to pay! (See Matthew 12:36.)

The reasons for the resurrection however need to be looked at.

📖 *Read: Acts 2:22-24. Here are found two reasons why He came back to life again.*

Firstly, because God the Father raised Him (see Ephesians 1:20). Secondly, because as He is the Eternal Son of God it is inevitable that He could not be contained by death. The 'mind blowing' thing is that He (God) allowed himself to be killed and buried in the first place!

Jesus' return to life was as real as His death and burial. It was not the return to life of a spirit, or an illusion, but the return of a person in a real body that could be touched, hugged and could eat food!

❓ **Question**: How many bits of evidence can you find in the four Biblical accounts of the bodily resurrection of Jesus (see above) that indicate *a real physical resurrection?*

The resurrection of Jesus was also the public sign of His acceptance by God the Father and a vindication of His sacrificial death. If He had not been raised from the dead it would have invalidated His sacrifice, disproved His Godhead and made Him incapable of saving us (see Romans 4:25 and 1 Corinthians 15:1-19).

## JESUS ROSE BODILY FROM THE GRAVE, SO WHERE IS JESUS NOW AND WHAT IS HE DOING?

The form and location of heaven has been the subject of much debate and humour. What we do know is that Jesus has promised that at the end of this age, God will produce a new heaven, a place for his followers to live with Him and the Father. Each age needs a model of heaven to believe in and to visualise. For those of New Testament times heaven was 'up there' in the sky. To us today, who can observe and record pictures of light from distant galaxies that appear to have been travelling for 12 billion years, we need a different picture, but in terms of our knowledge and understanding relative to that of God – an equally simple illustrative model or explanation.

A useful current explanation is that, in the same way as by turning a radio dial we can change the wavelength the set receives and can thus move from one station to another, similarly by changing the very 'frequency' of His creation, God can move from one form of His creation (what we know as Earth) to another where He, God, is (i.e. heaven)! But this is only a simple, inadequate explanation/illustration, not to be taken too seriously. What is clear, is that unlike the optimistic 'new start', 'we can do it', 'we can sort out the world's problems' messages of the new millennium celebrations, the Bible says very clearly that planet Earth will wear out and be replaced by God (see Psalm 102:25-27 and Hebrews 1:1-13). However it is the duty of all Christians to treat the world that God created with respect whilst it remains. (See Psalm 19:1.)

📖 *Read: John 20:17; Acts 1:1-11 especially verses 9-11. After His resurrection, Jesus physically ascended into the immediate heavenly presence of His Father.*

He ascended to the position of 'chief executive' of the Universe, to continue His work of bringing to full fruition all the plans of the Father. This involves at least three things:

1. He is responsible for giving the Holy Spirit to His people, as promised by the Father. (See John 7:37-39; Acts 1:8.)

2. He has authority to rule the Nations as King of Kings and Lord of Lords. (See 1 Corinthians 15:25; Ephesians 1:22-23 and Hebrews 10:12-13.)

3. In his new position at the Father's side, He presents Himself to the Father on our behalf, as our faithful and merciful representative in the courts of heaven. (See Hebrews 2:17-18; 4:14-16.)

? **Question**: What are the *two* essential qualifications of an effective representative (priesthood)?

So does this present state of affairs go on forever? No – but Jesus' reign will continue forever. More of that later in the next individual study.

# Week 9:
# THE HOLY SPIRIT AND THE SECOND COMING

## GROUP WORK SECTION

This week will consist of a brief discussion on how each member 'got on' with their individual tasks:

1. Prayer and fasting

2. Memory verse (1 Peter 3:18)

3. Individual study

Next, your study leader will go through last week's individual study entitled 'Jesus rose bodily from the dead – so what does it mean?' Each in turn will be asked to outline the answers they have given and the conclusions reached. This will involve some general discussion as the review proceeds.

The study leader will then outline the individual tasks for next week. They are:

1. The next individual Bible study, that will help you develop further your understanding of the function of the Holy Spirit and about Christ's second coming. Again, work through the next study and be ready to share your answers and conclusions next week.

2. Individual prayer target. Try and spend a minimum of 30 minutes each day in prayer. Remember to prepare a prayer list to help you use your prayer time effectively.

3. Again, try to fast for one day before the next group meeting. Focus your efforts around an issue such as praying for physical healing or an issue that is currently being faced by people in your church fellowship who you know.

4. Memorise Scripture for this week (1 Corinthians 2:12).

# INDIVIDUAL WORK SECTION

This section is for individual study. Your conclusions and answers will be discussed at the next group meeting, as will those of other group members.

When Jesus was alive, He told His disciples that *it was better* that He left them, because His Father (God) would send the Comforter (the Holy Spirit) via Jesus.

📖 *Read: John 1:32-34; John 3:6; John 14:15-31; Acts 2; Galatians 5:16-25 and Romans 8:1-27.*

❓ **Question**: So who or what is the Holy Spirit?

📖 *Read: Genesis 1:2; 41:38,39; Exodus 35:30-35; Judges 3:9-10; Psalm 51 (in particular verse 11).*

❓ **Question**: Was the Holy Spirit active in Old Testament times?

📖 *Read: Matthew 28:19; John 16:13-15 and Romans 8:9-11.*

❓ **Questions**: What evidence do we have for referring to the Holy Spirit as a person? What do these verses teach us about His, the Holy Spirit's relationship to the Father, to Jesus and to each individual Christian?

📖 *Read: John 16:8-11; 1 Thessalonians 1:5 and John 3:3-8.*

℁ **Questions**: What part does the Holy Spirit play in a person's conversion? What practical importance does this have for us as individuals and for the way we live our 'day-to-day' life – problems/challenges and all?

## HOW THE HOLY SPIRIT CAN HELP US TO LIVE OUR LIVES

> *I recall all you have done O Lord; I remember your wonderful deeds of long ago.*

A preacher once recounted the story that took place in a region of Mexico where hot and cold springs are found in close proximity. As a result local women use the hot springs to boil washing and the cold springs to rinse. One visitor remarked on how fortunate the women were for 'nature' to provide hot and cold water side by side and completely free! 'Not really,' one of the women replied, 'We have to provide the soap ... and there are machines in other parts of the world that do this sort of thing for you.'

On the other hand, for someone who already has a washing machine, they might be wanting this year's model, like the one belonging to a friend! As the preacher said, 'Contentment is not getting what you want but enjoying what you have.'

There is a clear principle here, if you *want* to be miserable, focus your thinking on what others have and forget what God has given you. *Comparing*, no matter who you are, will always leave you feeling left out, rejected or somehow 'short-changed'. It is important to stop this way of thinking; otherwise you will become negative and critical of every aspect of your life! In the Bible, an entire generation of the children of Israel died doing just that. The grumblers ended up going round a desert in circles. However the next generation, grateful to God for all He had done and had provided for them, entered the Promised Land, a land of blessing. (See Numbers: Chapters 11, 12, 14 and 16.)

An old Christian chorus talks about, *'Count your blessings, name them one by one ... and you will see what God has done.'* That is, list all that God has done for you. If you think hard you will be able to produce a very long list even if you are convinced (and maybe for very good reason) that you have had a bad deal out of life!

Now for the key point – if you reach the conclusion, no matter how reluctantly, that your attitude is 'not good' -after a time of prayer, repentance and waiting on God – if you will let him, and if you ask, He will fill you with the Holy Spirit to transform your mind, attitudes and, as a result, your life! In Ezekiel God describes The Holy Spirit as a river flowing from His throne.

📖 *Read: Ezekiel 47. See how the narrator went deeper and deeper into the river (a picture of the Holy Spirit), until out of his depth.*

As Brother Ramon, an Anglican Franciscan friar and hermit, puts it;

> *The same Spirit who raises the sap in the trees in springtime, who turns the cycle of the seasons, who causes the rising and the setting of the sun and the waxing and waning of the moon ... this is the Spirit sent by Jesus, to flow not only into the world of nature, but into the (human) experience of Grace ... the source of the Spirit is the Throne and Altar of God in the Temple ... the symbol of God's loving heart – and the river flows, renewing and enlightening ... as the believer opens his or her*

*heart to such Spiritual indwelling ... the river flows*
*in and through and out ... in thirst-quenching*
*fertilising and verdant beauty, to the whole world*
*around.*

In Ezekiel 47 God describes stages of experience of the Holy Spirit. Most Christians experience the in-flowing of the Holy Spirit as a result of prayer (communion with God). So a deepening prayer life will lead to a deepening experience of the Holy Spirit. The stages:

1. *Ankle-deep (Ez. 47:2-3)*. This is the stage when at the beginning of a life of prayer. It is like being on a beach at the edge of a large ocean, where waves pound in carrying messages from the great depths. If ankle-deep, then prayer/communion with the Father, through the Son and in the power of the Holy Spirit, is **prayer of petition**. That is prayer centring on needs, concerns and usually around oneself and immediate family or friends.

2. *Knee-deep (Ez. 47:4a)*. Often when bathing on a beach, moving out from paddling at the edge into deeper water is usually gradual. However moving from being ankle-deep to knee-deep may not be a big jump forward, but it is real progress and shows determination in terms of moving into deeper water. By contrast, knee-deep praying is the developing of a greater awareness and concern for those who cannot pray for themselves – the beginning of what is called **intercessory prayer**. Intercessory prayer is not about pleading with a reluctant God to grant favours to an unworthy human. It is rather individuals involved in the healing energies of the Holy Spirit on behalf of sick and sinful men and women and across the whole of our planet! It will involve praying for friends, those not known to us personally and our enemies – yes, our enemies too!

3. *Waist-deep (Ez.47:4b).* This depth of water is now getting deep. Communion with the Father, through the Son and in the power of the Holy Spirit at this stage involves **prayers of gratefulness, praise and adoration**, allowing the love of God to flow over and around you, as you rest/float in Him. But waist-deep water becomes out-of-depth water, in terms of communion with the Holy Spirit (prayer) and meditation – a form of meditation that is very different from that of the eastern religions or current New Age thinking. It is also the feeling of sinfulness and unworthiness when so close to the presence of God. (See Luke 5:4-8.)

4. *Out of your depth (Ez. 47:5).* This sort of prayer can be scary, as can swimming out of your depth! Such **prayers by invitation/intervention of the Spirit**, are open to all, but involves allowing you to be taken by the Spirit into the deeper water to allow greater communion with the Father through the Son. This area of prayer also involves warfare between the powers of darkness and the consuming fire of God's holiness and love. As Brother Ramon says: *'Only over the last few years have I begun to allow myself to be taken by the Holy Spirit into the deeper waters. It is scary, it is overwhelming, but it is inevitable for those who are seeking the depths of God the Father's loving mystery.'*

5. *The continuous experience (Ez. 47:12).* If a young, or an older, Christian begins this journey of being **increasingly filled with the Holy Spirit through a life of prayer**, then as each progresses, the water becomes deeper and the effect on us is loving, gentle but dramatic. Our egocentric prayer 'shopping lists' give way to a deeper awareness of God the Father's love and His purposeful activity, that is, as we become more tuned into His will. When this happens, we will receive from Him an awareness of His compassion and His healing, not just for ourselves but for others. It will

involve weeping for the lost, for those damaged by life's experiences and rejoicing over everyone who experiences 'new life in Jesus'.

Jesus called the Holy Spirit 'Comforter' or 'Advocate' or 'Councillor'. (See John 14:26 – the word means 'someone called alongside to help'.)

📖 *Read: John 16:12-15; 1 Corinthians 2:8-12; Galatians 5:22-25; Acts 1:8 and Romans 8:26-27.*

❓ **Question**: What are some of the ways in which the Holy Spirit can help a Christian?

## HOW SHOULD THIS HELP FROM THE HOLY SPIRIT BE WORKING OUT IN OUR OWN LIVES AND IN OUR CHURCH?

The Holy Spirit is often and has traditionally been referred to as '(Holy) Comforter'. Words change their meaning over time. For example, in the Bayeux tapestry in Bayeux Cathedral, France, produced in 11th Century Normandy to record the events of and commemorate the Battle of Hastings, King Harold is shown 'comforting' his troops. The 'comfort' consists of prodding his troops with a sharp spear in the backside to 'encourage' them to fight harder! We therefore need to give the word 'comforter' a wider meaning: it can mean, 'spur into action', 're-energise', 'goad', 'encourage'. This is in addition to the more obvious current meaning of the word 'comforter', of a 'soothing' granny patting a distressed child on the head and telling him or her that 'it will be all right'!

Jesus will reign forever! He will continue to rule from Heaven until God the Father is satisfied that the objectives of Jesus' death and resurrection have been achieved.

📖 *Read: 1 Corinthians 15:20-28, note especially v.25. Jesus must reign until He has put all His Father's enemies under His feet – that is until they have been utterly defeated. Then Jesus will return to Earth.*

In the Bible we are told that this return of Jesus will take the world by surprise – but *not* His own people.

📖 *Read: 1 Thessalonians 5:1-6. There will be worldwide public signs of His coming and the believers will be waiting and ready!*

This principle is clearly described in the story of the ten bridesmaids.

📖 *Read: Matthew 25:1-13. It should be noted that a large part of the Bible, in particular the New Testament, deals with Jesus' second coming.*

## JESUS WILL COME AGAIN – SOME BIBLICAL FACTS ABOUT THE FUTURE

Currently there are in society two contradictory attitudes towards the future. One view is that we must think more about it, the other less! The first group, the 'optimists' or futurologists, sees us living in a world of swiftly accelerating change. In every walk of life the effects of change are felt. For example, currently knowledge doubles every 9-10 years. All over the world 'think tanks' and research groups are trying to grapple with the enormous problems facing our planet. Futurologists believe our only hope is to keep one step ahead. This view was very evident during the celebrations for the new millennium and in the spoken 'platitudes' of world leaders.

145

The second group, the 'pessimists' believe 'doomsday' to be just around the corner – less than 25 years away. They suggest that there is little man can do about it. Further, they suggest we should all turn our backs on the future and concentrate on the present or past. So existentialism (living for the present) and nostalgia (living for a largely mythical past golden age) are both currently popular themes and deeply ingrained in our culture.

## THE IMMEDIATE FUTURE

The Bible calls the immediate future 'this present evil age'. It paints a clear and increasingly familiar picture of the world in the final days:

1. *Personal life style* – pleasure for its own sake, repudiation of authority, growth in lawlessness, violence, immorality of every kind will increase, family life will break up and traditional values and social norms turned on their head.

2. *Political* – democracy will gradually give way to forms of dictatorship even in the Western democracies. There will be great efforts for peace that will fail. *So watch Jerusalem and events in the Middle East!*

The Bible reveals that there will be changes in a number of areas. They are:

1. *Ecclesiastical* – the official church will be marked by compromise and weakness leading to one united 'world church'. There could even be a coming together of all the word religions. Cults will multiply often within the world's terms – with outstanding leaders. There will be a blurring of the line between church and world.

2. *Natural* – earthquakes, floods, other major disasters and

scorching heat. Pollution will become an ever-greater problem.

3. *Spiritual* – worldwide evangelism will mark the last days. The result of this will largely be ridicule, opposition, scoffing and outright persecution of Christian believers by much of the rest of the world, though many will listen and become Christians.

This will all lead to what the Bible calls the 'Big Trouble' or the 'Great Tribulation'. This is described in the books of Daniel, Matthew, 2 Thessalonians and Revelation. There are prophecies in these books that a confederacy of ten kingdoms, probably in the Mediterranean/Middle East area, will become a new 'super power'. Three rulers will be replaced by one dominant figure. The Bible calls this person the 'antichrist' (instead of Christ). This new godless world rule will lead to what the Bible calls the final cataclysm of the Great Tribulation.

There are two views involving Christians and the Great Tribulation. There is general agreement amongst Biblical scholars that Jews will unfortunately have to live through it – but will Christians?

1. The 'classical view' is that the Christians will have to live through this terrible time.

2. The 'rapture' view is that they will be 'raptured', that is snatched away before the Tribulation, in a way similar to the shelter God provided for Noah at the time of the Flood and with the Passover in Egypt for the Jews. This is the idea of the 'protection' of the faithful 'remnant' as seen during the captivity/exile period of Jewish history from abut 590 BC, a consistent theme in the Bible. Many biblical scholars believe that this was broadly the view held by the New Testament Church.

## THE AGE THAT IS TO COME

The antichrist will be the world's second to last ruler – Jesus Christ will be the last and final ruler of the world! During the final World War (directed at Israel), at its height, Jesus will return to His land Israel and to His capital Jerusalem. *This event is referred to over 300 times in the Bible.*

However, there is a difference of opinion amongst Christians about where and when Christ will set up His Kingdom. Also about whether this thousand-year 'millennium' will *follow* or *precede* His return.

Three views exist:

1. *Pre-millennial view* – this 'building the kingdom' and thousand-year rule will take place after Christ's return. Jesus will build His Kingdom. This view incorporates a central role for both Christians, Jews and for Israel. This was the view broadly held by the New Testament Church and is the traditional biblical view.

2. *Post-millennial view* – this view believes that *the Church* will build the Kingdom of Christ by 'Christianising' the whole world *before* Jesus returns. As a new convert is made they argue, so the Kingdom is built (increased). This view sees no special place for either Jews (other than via normal conversion) or any significance in the establishment of modern Israel as the fulfilment of biblical prophecy, or in the current return to it of millions of Jews from all over the world. This was a view popular at the time of the Pilgrim Fathers' journey from England to America. For many of them, the aim was a fresh start away from corrupt satanic Europe, religious persecution and the building in 'The New World', a religious state/society on biblical principles.

3. *A-millennial view* – this view is widely held in the 'established

148

church'. It sees the 'millennium' concept as a spiritual experience, rather than an actual event. The thousand-year reign is seen simply seen as a spiritual picture.

It is important that we understand what the Bible has to say about Jesus' return. Much of it is clear and thus above the sort of debate outlined above. The important thing is to be like the wise bridesmaids – ready for the return of Jesus. Although it is good to have a view, what is far more important, is that there is much that all three of the above views can agree on.

📖 *Read: Matthew 24:26; Mark 13:26-27; Luke 12:35-40; John 12:37-50; 14:1-4; Acts 1:1-10; 1 Corinthians 15:51-57; 1Thessalonians 4:16-17; 1 Peter 4:7-8; 2 Peter 3:8-13 and Revelation 22:20-21.*

❓ **Question**: Can you identify in the above passages at least ten principles or facts about His return that help you understand the events better?

## BUT WHAT ABOUT CHRISTIANS?

📖 *Read: 1 Corinthians 15:50-53 and 1 Thessalonians 4:17. If we are alive on earth when Jesus comes back we shall be 'caught up' and 'changed' – that is given new bodies.*

If we have died previously, this includes all Christians who have already passed on, our spirits will be with the Lord and we shall return with Jesus and be 'changed'.

📖 *Read: 1 Thessalonians 4:13-18.*

## AND WHAT ABOUT NON-CHRISTIANS?

This is a difficult one, so we should let the Bible speak for itself.

📖 *Read: 2 Peter 3:1-10. This describes the fate of the earth and of those who remain on it.*

📖 *Read: Matthew 13:36-50; 25:46; Revelation 20:11-15 and Daniel 12:1-3.*

Sadly there is one clear and inescapable conclusion. Jesus is desperately sad about it too, that is after all why He came into this world, suffered and died! All the above references speak of eternal judgement and assignment to Hell, of those who reject Jesus. Hell is a *permanent* separation from God and all that is good. There is no reprieve. For some time many church leaders have tried to dismiss or diminish what the Bible says about Hell. Some for very understandable reasons have sought refuge from the uncomfortable picture the Bible clearly paints, by talking about only the most evil going to Hell. Others have chosen to seek refuge in unbiblical notions of annihilation for those who do not go to Heaven.

## WHAT CAN WE LEARN ABOUT HELL FROM THE BIBLE?

📖 *Read: Psalm 86:13; Matthew 8:12; Matthew 25:41; Romans 1:18-20; 2 Peter 2:4-9; Jude 1:7 and Revelation 21:8.*

📖 *Read: Matthew 5; 10:28; 18:9; Mark 9; Luke 12:5; 16:23; James 3:6 and 2 Peter 2:4.*

✼ **Questions**:

1. Given what the Bible says about Hell, and it is uncomfortable, what should the Christian response be?

2. In the light of what the Bible says about Hell, what does it tell us about Jesus' death and His commission before ascending to be with the Father?

3. What can we learn about Heaven from the Bible?

📖 *Read: Isaiah 25:8; Matthew 5:17-20; 7:13-14; John 14:2-3; 2 Corinthians 5:2; Philippians 1:23; Colossians 3:1-5; 2 Peter 3:13; Revelation 7:1; 21:4 and 22:5.*

## THE CHRISTIANS AFTER JESUS' RETURN

📖 *Read: Revelation 21:1-8. All of the old system has passed away with the end of the age.*

We are in reality given very little information in Scripture about Heaven, Hell, or life beyond the end of this age. The glimpses we do have of the 'New Heaven' and the 'New Earth' and the warnings by Jesus concerning the awful reality of God's wrath, judgement and eternal destruction, should be sufficient to make us desire the one and flee from the other. That is God's intention.

We do know that once the judgement has taken place, there is no appeal and no purgatory after which we may change places. (See Luke 16:23-26.)

*JESUS LIVES AND REIGNS FOREVER AND WE*
*SHALL LIVE AND REIGN WITH HIM*
*FOREVER*

## FURTHER READING

If you wish to study further the prophecies about end-time events, the following books are recommended:

Pawson David, *When Jesus Returns*, Hodder & Stoughton, London.

Pawson D., *Explaining the Second Coming*, Sovereign World, ISBN: 1852401184.

Pawson D., (1999), *Hope for the Millennium*, Hodder and Stoughton, ISBN 0340735597.

Miller E.J., *The Final Battle*, New Wine Press.

Walvoord J.F., *Armageddon Oil and the Middle East Crisis*, Zondervan.

La Haye T., *The Beginning of the End*, Tyndale.

La Haye T, Jenkins S, (1998), *Left Behind*, Tyndale, ISBN: 0842329110.

# Week 10:
# THE RELEVANCE OF
# THE BIBLE AND OTHER
# PRACTICAL MATTERS

## INTRODUCTION TO THE CONCLUDING STUDY

This is the last week of the series of studies and will be slightly different in structure from the previous few weeks. It will probably last a little longer.

It will have these main components:

1. The usual review by your study leader of last week's individual study regarding the Holy Spirit and the Second Coming. The review will follow the normal pattern that has been established including the memory verses.

2. A short group Bible study led by the study leader, that will bring together all the studies and suggest a way forward.

3. A time to discuss the series of studies, identify what you have got out of it and decide some action points for the future.

4. Guidelines for group leaders and prospective group leaders.

Now that you have experienced the self-study approach to Bible study, structured prayer, fasting and the concept of memorising verses of Scripture, it is hoped that you will have learned a little about the essential ingredients for the Normal Christian Life!

A short series such as this can only just scratch the surface. It can only reveal a glimpse of what is there in Scripture awaiting discovery under the direction of the Holy Spirit! The Apostle Paul describes the Normal Christian Life as running a race and the Christian as an athlete. So, be like an Olympic athlete, start training in earnest – God has a gold medal (or far better) waiting at the end of the race. Keep going until you reach the winning post! Do not be distracted to the right or the left; do not look back.

## GROUP WORK SECTION

In the introduction to the series it was suggested that the Bible has something useful to say about how we should live our lives in the 21st Century. It was also stated in the introduction that the Bible is God's 'workshop manual' or 'maker's instructions' for life – every aspect of it.

To experience God's solutions to life's problems, it is important for each of us to walk closely with God and become more like Him. We must pray regularly, worship with other Christians regularly and read the Bible regularly (1 Peter 2:2-3).

So we will therefore conclude this series with a look at the Bible itself.

But first this week will consist of a brief discussion on how each member 'got on' with their individual tasks:

1. Prayer and fasting

2. Memory verse

3. Individual study (1 Corinthians 2:12).

Next, we must briefly go through last week's individual study on the Holy Spirit and the Second Coming. Each in turn should outline the answers they have given and the conclusions reached.

Then we turn to a group study on the relevance of the Bible.

## WHAT EXACTLY IS THE BIBLE?

📖 Read: Exodus 32:15-16; 2 Samuel 23:2; Acts 1:16; 2 Timothy 3:16; 2 Peter 1:21.

? **Question**: What does the Bible say about its own authorship – both Old and New Testament?

📖 *Read: Matthew 5:17-19; John 10:34-36; Luke 24:25-27, 44.*

? **Question**: What was the approach of Jesus to the Old Testament?

📖 *Read: Matthew 4:3,4; Luke 4:16-21; Acts 2:16-36; Acts 8:30-35.*

? **Question**: In what way did Jesus and the early church use the Old Testament?

📖 *Read: John 20:30-31; 2 Thessalonians 3:14; 2 Peter 3:15-16; Revelation 1:1-3.*

? **Question**: How did the Apostles view their own writing?

📖 *Read: John 14:25-26; 16:12-14.*

? **Question**: How do the comments that Jesus made about the Holy Spirit relate to this?

📖 *Read: 2 Timothy 3:15,16; Romans 10:17; 15:4; Psalm 119:9; Ephesians 6:17.*

? **Question**: Why bother reading the Bible? What should we expect to get from it?

📖 *Read: 1 Thessalonians 2:13; 1 Timothy 4:13; Acts 17:11; Psalm 119:11-16.*

? **Question**: In what way should we approach the Bible?

📖 *Read: 1 Corinthians 2:8-14; John 16:12-14.*

? **Question**: What is the one vital factor in understanding the Bible?

To summarise this section let us go right back to one of the very first statements made in the introduction to this series and rephrase it as a question.

? **Question**: How does the teaching of the Bible apply to today's problems?' Give examples from the following readings.

📖 *Read: 2 Kings 22:8-20; Psalm 119:1-88; Psalm 119:89-176; Luke 4:16-29; 2 Timothy 3:14-17; 2 Peter 1:12-21.*

? **Question**: How would you explain your answer to an adult neighbour, or to a child between 10 and 12?

You will see from reading the above that Scripture, the inspired word of God, is the key to dealing with the trials, pressures and problems of modern life. It gives a formula for success and key principles for handling life. Therefore Scripture, its study and the right approach to it are vital. It should be remembered that the Trinity however is Father, Son and Holy Spirit and not Father Son and Holy Scripture!

℘    **Question**: How can I be sure to get the place of Scripture in my life and my attitude to it correct?

## REACTONS TO THE WORK OF THE HOLY SPIRIT

A final comment: In Acts 2:6-13 we read about the reaction of non-believers to the movement of the Holy Spirit. In this story we have three very clear group reactions:

Group 1: The disciples and other believers; these were very different men and women from what they had been just a few days or hours earlier! No longer were they fearful or cowardly. No longer were they a patient, hoping, praying group. Now they were bold, powerful, anointed preachers and witnesses to what Jesus had done for them!

Group 2: The crowd, bewildered, astonished, amazed and puzzled at hearing such wonderful words of hope, each in his or her mother tongue! Many would become part of the crowd of three thousand, who responded to the Spirit's call in Peter's preaching.

Group 3: The remainder, the threatened, the critical, the disbelieving who sneered at the disciples and sought to put them down with such cheap but calculated insults as *'Oh they have been drinking'* or *'I wonder what they are on?'*

In reading again the great commission of Jesus before He ascended to the Father (Acts 1:8), we in group 1 have a duty to ensure that 'the world' has a chance of being in group 2!

Regrettably, there will be many, many that will elect to join group 3. However, we in group 1 have an obligation from Jesus to give all of mankind a chance of joining group 2 and thereby group 1.

?   **Questions**:

1. What can and should I do to obey the commission of Jesus in Acts 1:8?

2. Where should each of us begin?

3. How can I draw up an action plan?

4. What ways are best (for me) of telling others what Jesus has done in my life? That is, how Jesus is helping me to cope with the ups and downs of life.

## REVIEW TIME

Now review any matters of this 10-week course which require group discussion before considering prospects of future leadership.

# Notes

## PRACTICAL MATTERS FOR CELL GROUP LEADERS AND POTENTIAL LEADERS: GUIDANCE NOTES

In leading an ESG cell group it is important to give each participant space to explore issues for themselves. Allow plenty of debate, at times perhaps 'rigorous debate', which can be helpful. However the object of the groups is to learn from God using His revelation in the Bible. It is not for individuals to propagate their own philosophies or prejudices. Make sure that the end result is 'learning from God' with the help of the Holy Spirit and not just an airing of personal views and ideas! Thus it is suggested that before each meeting you as leader spend some considerable time in prayer seeking wisdom, an anointing and good judgement from God. Pray for each participant individually, seeking wisdom about how to help him or her in their quest to know God better.

### A NEW CELL GROUP COURSE

When putting together a new course seek those wanting to learn from the Bible about God. Often and sadly, badly run cell groups can in reality achieve little more than a pooling of ignorance! It is important to try and put together a group from say 6 to 10 in number, where typically all are relatively new Christians. In principle it is good to mix age, education and social background. However, wisdom gained from prayer is the key here. Let that guide any decision that you have to make.

### RUNNING A MEETING

It is important to set time targets, that is to ensure that a meeting finishes at a sensible agreed time – on time. Provide structure by breaking the meeting up in your mind into sections and finish each by a certain target time. Agree an overall meeting duration at the first meeting, as some may have issues of 'baby sitters', late night transport and early work starts the next morning.

Start the meeting with a short time of prayer and, if you have a musician, one or two (only) praise songs. Then get stuck in – leave the refreshments to the end – but ensure there is a time at the end for the refreshments and a friendly chat.

Develop a method of maintaining discipline, with nobody hogging the discussion and one person talking at a time. When going through the individual studies with the group, draw out but don't embarrass or pressure people into comments, particularly if you detect reluctance to share. This will probably resolve itself as confidence increases and friendships grow. Ensure that you manage to speak individually to each member, even if only by phone or e-mail during the individual study period each week. This is particularly important during the first three or four weeks. A small cosy room in someone's home is often better than a large, cold, mainly empty church hall as the venue for the cell group meeting.

**FOLLOW-UP**

When week 10 finally arrives and passes, for many of the group it will leave an anticlimax. Hopefully they have enjoyed coming and have found the study personally stimulating and challenging.

It is important as cell group leader to do two things:

1. Discuss with each where they are on their spiritual journey, perhaps pray with them over issues, or refer them to a church leader or to another Christian with suitable skills or experience.

2. Discuss with them 'what next' – help them to develop a realistic personal development plan. You should encourage each to lead a cell group him- or herself using the ESG course material. Do this whilst the enthusiasm is still high; if necessary offer and give support/moral encouragement, particularly for the first couple of weeks. Perhaps help them (gently) to put a new group together. But let them make the decisions, by seeking God and then trusting the answers that they get. Your job is to 'be there' for support only. Spiritually they have to come of age.

Try and keep in touch with each of the cell group members until you are sure that each is 'functioning well'. If there are a few having problems perhaps a 'one-off' reunion may help. Resist any pressure to form a permanent group, or you may find yourself running not a cell group but an institution locked in time! Confidence will likely be a major issue: try and ensure dependence is centred on God alone through prayer. Clearly there is a role for one-to-one or group support and in addition to be an active member in a live functioning church; but there is a danger that 'new Christians' can place dependence on a person, their elder, cell group leader etc. This should be avoided – *point them to Jesus and His Father every time*.

## FOR THOSE WHO HAVE JUST COMPLETED AN ESG COURSE

## SO WHAT NEXT?

Firstly congratulations – you have successfully completed a cell group course and should have a much clearer idea about what you believe, how to study the Bible, prayer and all the essential activities necessary for finding *God's Solutions to Life's Problems*.

## THE 'ESCALATOR PRINCIPLE'

The *Essential Survival Guide* is in some ways at least a bit like going up an escalator the wrong way (one that is going down). If you do not go forward, making clear progress, you will go backwards, and sometimes very quickly. All the progress you have made will then be lost. In the *Essential Survival Guide* you cannot stand still – you are either going forward or going backwards. So beware of taking a 'rest' or of becoming complacent: all are ploys of Satan!

## KEEP GOING FORWARD

There are three things you must do to keep going forward. They are:

1. Ensure that you have a regular 'quiet time' every day, preferably first thing in the morning! This should be a minimum of half an hour, split between Bible study and prayer. If you can only manage half an hour in the morning, try and ensure that you have a second formal prayer time at the end of the day. Other prayer times are possible, for example on buses, trains and at lunchtime.

2. Undertake a serious deeper personal Bible study several times a week. It can be helpful to use, over several weeks, a study book on one of the Gospels or on a Bible character. Your church leader should be able to help you here. Make sure you chose a study book by an author who accepts the whole Bible as the inspired word of God. Avoid books by those who criticise or dismiss the parts of the Bible that they don't like, or that don't fit in to their personal 'world-view'.

3. Join and take an active part in your local church. Seek companionship from those who are hungrily studying 'the word of God'. Seek God's confirmation through prayer and practical signs that this is the right church for you.

Finally, as many teachers will tell you, the best way to learn a subject is to teach it! This is an important principle, as the person who led the *Essential Survival Guide* cell group that you attended, probably learned more from running it than you did from attending! So get started, help set up the next one and run it yourself – yes, you run one! The Holy Spirit has already given you all the gifts/skills that you need. You need to just start using them! Aim to have it running within a couple of weeks of the finish of the one you attended. Stick to the principles you tried and tested throughout the ten weeks of the *Essential Survival Guide*. Read the notes for cell group leaders from your own perspective and consult the person who led your group about your feelings and intentions.

## SO GET STARTED!

The key thing is to get started and quickly – remember the story of the wise bridesmaids (Matthew 25:1-13). We really don't know when the Lord will return! Recommended further personal reading material that is very practical and will help you in your personal Christian life. It is recommended that you read the books in the following order:

1. Urquhart, Colin (1990), *My Dear Child*, Hodder & Stoughton, London, ISBN 0 - 340 53642 - X.

2. Urquhart, Colin (1992), *My Dear Son*, Hodder & Stoughton, London, ISBN 0 - 340 55809 - 1.

3. Urquhart, Colin (2000), *My Beloved*, London, Marshall Pickering/Harper Collins, ISBN 0 - 551 03263 - 4.

## A PRAYER FOR WHEN LIFE GETS TOUGH!

When life is tough for a time – the words below may help as a prayer or a song if the Holy Spirit gives you a tune.

*Thank you Lord, that you are so wonderful!*

*Your love is never-ending.*

*Let all who belong to you say: Your love is never-ending.*

*Let all with leadership responsibility in the Kingdom of God say: Your love is never-ending.*

*Let all who fear you say: Your love is never-ending.*

*When overwhelmed with life's problems I prayed to Jesus*

*And He answered me and rescued me.*

*Jesus is taking care of me.*

*So I will not fear about what will happen.*

*What in the final analysis can other human beings really do to me?*

*Yes, Jesus is providing solutions for me.*

*I will dismiss as unimportant those who wish to bring me down.*

*Trusting Jesus is the key – not other people.*

*Trusting Jesus is the key – not trusting the powerful, the self-opinionated or the famous.*

*Despite the fact that I was surrounded by a number of major problems, all were resolved in the name of Jesus.*

*Yes they overwhelmed me, got under my skin for a time, but I overcame each one of them in the name of Jesus and in the power of the Holy Spirit.*

*They buzzed around my brain like bees.*

*They were as damaging as a fire out of control!*

*Nevertheless, I overcame each one of them in the name of Jesus.*

*Satan, Lucifer, you did your best to crush me, yes even to kill me.*

*But Jesus came to my rescue – Hallelujah!*

*Jesus is my strength alone.*

*He puts His peace and a song of joy in my heart.*

*In Jesus alone is my victory.*

*Jesus, those who belong to your kingdom just want to spend time in your presence singing praises to you!*

*The Holy Spirit has done some amazing things.*

*The Holy Spirit is moving amongst us to bring Glory to the Father – God.*

*The Holy Spirit has done amazing things!*

*I will rise up from a feeling of defeat with drive and energy to embrace all that the Lord has done!*

*All that He is doing...*

*Yes Jesus has corrected me, forgiven me and challenged me to the core of my being.*

*But has never deserted me because He loves me!*

*In my praise to the Father and to the Son Jesus I will come into the very presence of God.*

*By this means I and other believers can touch spiritually the robe of Jesus and receive healing.*

*I thank you Jesus for answering all my prayers and bringing me to a place of victory.*

*The person that the world has repeatedly said was useless has become a key servant of God!*

*This is the Lord's doing!*

*Yes and He does it for so many of us.*

*It is so wonderful that it brings tears to my eyes!*

*This is another day from the Father.*

*I will rejoice because today He will give me victory in many, many areas.*

*Bless all the things I do today, Lord.*

*Praise and glory to Jesus who comes in the name of God the Father.*

*All honour and praise from those in Your Kingdom here on earth.*

*Let us put the fruit of the Spirit that our lives are producing on an altar as an offering to the Father.*

*Jesus you are my Lord, my God, and I will praise You.*

*You are my God and I will worship You.*

*Thank you Jesus because you are the perfect Friend.*

*You just don't stop **loving each one of us!***

(Based around Psalm 118)